To Kill a

G000094818

By Stan Abbott

The run-down of the Settle-Carlisle line; the endeavours of 22,265 people and a dog to prevent its closure and the relevance of it all to transport policy in Britain.

Cover graphics by Harry Hammill. Picture by Barry Wilkinson/ Picture House.

in assocation with

WEST YORKSHIRE
Metropolitan County Council

THIS BOOK IS DEDICATED TO ALL THOSE CAMPAIGNING AGAINST THE
STATUS QUO IN PURSUIT OF A BETTER DEAL FOR ORDINARY PEOPLE

To Kill a Railway

First impression, February 1986

Published by Leading Edge Press and Publishing, The Watchmaker's,
Town Head, Hawes, North Yorkshire, DL8 3RG. Tel. (096 97) 566.

© 1986 Stan Abbott

This book is copyright under the Berne convention. All rights are
reserved. Apart from any fair dealing for research, private study or
review as permitted under the Copyright Act, 1956, no part of this
publication may be reproduced, stored in a retrieval system, or
transmitted in any form or by any means electronic, mechanical,
photocopying, recording or otherwise, without the permission of the
copyright holder.

British Library Cataloguing in Publication Data

Abbott, Stan
  To Kill a Railway
  1. Settle & Carlisle Railway -- History   2. British
  Rail, *London Midland Region*   -- History
  I. Title
  385'.09427   HE3020.S4

  ISBN   0-948135-01-8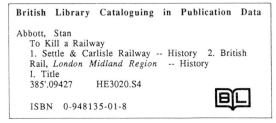

Design: Stan Abbott (Journalism)

This book is composed on an Apple Macintosh 512K computer, with
type processed by Designed Publications Ltd., 8-10 Trafford Road,
Alderley Edge, Cheshire, SK9 7NT.

Origination and printing by Impression, 14 Brown Lane West, Leeds,
LS12 6BH.

Author's note

BOOKS about the Settle to Carlisle railway have proliferated to such an extent in recent years that authors tend to begin by excusing themselves for adding to the numerous volumes already weighing down the railway buff's bookshelf. I make no apologies for attempting, in To Kill a Railway, to create a book of interest to a broad section of readers somewhere between the confirmed railway fanatic and the social scientist. It does not attempt to retell in detail the history of this remarkable living (as I write) monument to Victorian vision and engineering: some of the many excellent works dedicated to this aim are listed in the bibliography. Rather, the intention is to explain the fate of the Settle-Carlisle line in the context of political forces that have shaped Britain's railways since the 1930s. If, in so doing, the book stimulates discussion and promotes action to counter the vested interests which have locked our public transport into a spiral of decline, then perhaps its aim will have been achieved.

To Kill a Railway was originally conceived some time ago as a much weightier tome which never saw the light of day. The book you now read was born out of discussions with **West Yorkshire Metropolitan County Council's** Public Transport Committee Chairman Wayne Jenkins and the head of the county's Public Transport Office, John Carr. It is, hopefully, of more immediate relevance than my original idea and I am indebted to the county council, without whose financial assistance the project would not have been possible. I also owe it to the county council for, albeit unwittingly, imposing the sort of tight deadlines which ensure things get done. With the two transport users' consultative committees concerned due to hold their hearings into British Rail's closure plans in March and April 1986, and the demise of the county under controversial Government legislation expected soon afterwards, our decision in principle last October to go ahead with the project did not leave much time for writing! It should be added that my own views as expressed in this book are not necessarily those of the county council or its officers.

Stan Abbott, Hawes, January 1986

Acknowledgements

THE author is grateful for the advice and assistance of many people in writing this book. Particular thanks are due to John Carr, Head of West Yorkshire County Council's Public Transport Office, whose invaluable help was readily forthcoming at a difficult time for the authority when his other commitments were almost overwhelming; to County Councillors Wayne Jenkins and Andrew Jarosz; to Colin Speakman and John Whitelegg for their advice on the manuscript; to Bill Lehan for the cartoons and Ruth Abbott for the other graphics; to Lancaster Computing for their excellent back-up; to Yorkshire Post Newspapers for the use of their cuttings library; to the staff at the North Yorkshire branch library at Hawes for their patience in ordering many obscure titles; to all those who interrupted busy schedules to make time to be interviewed or to chase up information; and to all the moles within British Rail and official bodies everywhere who help cast light on the workings of Government.

Contents

v

Bibliography

An opinion of the Yorkshire Dales rail service in 1975, A.O. Grigg and P.G. Smith, Transport and Road Research Laboratory 1977

Bring back the trains: the case for railway reopenings, Railway Development Society, 1983

British Rail: a European railway, Transport 2000, March 1984

British Rail: an action plan, Transport 2000

British Railways Boad, corporate plan, 1985

Closure of the Settle-Carlisle railway line, The, J.S. Whitelegg, 1984

Dalesrail: a report of an experimental project in the Yorkshire Dales National Park, Countryside Commission 1979

Development of the major railway trunk routes, The, British Railways Board, 1965

Economic evaluation comparability study: the application of the SACTRA framework and COBA principles to railway investment, Colin Buchanan and partners, Department of Transport, 1984

Future of rural railways, The, Policy Studies Institute 1981

How to fight a rail cut, Railway Development Society, 1982

Hundred years of railway Weighells, A, Sidney Weighell, Robson Books

Interpreting the heritage of the Settle-Carlisle line, Manchester Polytechnic Centre for Environmental Interpretation, July 1985

Leisure, transport and the countryside, David Rubinstein, Colin Speakman, Fabian Society, 1969

Losing Track, Kerry Hamilton and Stephen Potter, Routledge and Kegan Paul in association with Channel 4, 1985

The Metro report, Metro Monitoring and Development Study (Transport and Road Research Laboratory, University of Newcastle, Tyne and Wear council, Tyne and Wear PTE)

Modernisation and re-equipment of British Railways, British Transport Commission, 1955

North of Leeds: the Settle-Carlisle line and its branches, Peter E. Baughan, Roundhouse 1966

Paying heed, Transport 2000, 1984

Rails in the fells, David Jenkinson, Peco 1973

Railway policy between the wars, Michael R. Bonavia, Manchester University Press, 1981

Railways in the Yorkshire Dales, K. Hoole, Dalesman 1978 (2nd impression)

Report of the Advisory Committee on Trunk Road Assessment, chairman Sir George Leitch, HMSO, 1977

Reshaping of British Railways, The, HMSO, 1963

Road building and the urban economy, J. Whitelegg. To be published by Transport 2000 in Cities and Roads conference report, 1986

Roads to Prosperity? Friends of the Earth

Rural railways and rural structures, J. Whitelegg, to be published in Regional Studies journal, 1986

Settle-Carlisle centenary, 1876-1976, British Rail 1976

Settle to Carlisle: a railway over the Pennines, W.R. Mitchell and David Joy, Dalesman

Settle to Carlisle in Colour, Dalesman

Settle and Carlisle railway, The, PEIDA, in association with W.A. Fairhurst and Partners

Settle & Carlisle railway: proposal for a feasability study.....Sian Johnson and Associates

Social consequences of rail closures, The, Mayer Hillman and Anne Whalley, Policy Studies Institute 1980

Story of the Settle-Carlisle line, The, Frederick W. Houghton and W. Hubert Foster, Norman Arch 1948

Transport Users' Consultative Committee, Yorkshire Area, annual reports 1981-84, North-Western Area, annual reports 1983 and 1984-5

Wayfarer project, The, Countryside Commission

Wensleydale railway, The, C.S. Hallas, Dalesman

Yorkshire Dales National Park Plan: review and draft for consultation, YDNP Committee

Your local trains in the 80s, Railway Development Society, 1979

Additional sources -- Press cuttings, various, particularly Modern Railways magazine, the Yorkshire Post, New Civil Engineer, Cambrian Coast Action Group bulletin and such other publications and television sources as mentioned in the test.

Foreword

THE Settle to Carlisle railway from its birth has achieved the seemingly impossible -- in engineering and scenic terms it is one of Britain's wonders. And now, under the threat of death, the line is awakening a new spirit.

During the past four years many lessons have been learned -- this book highlights them and hopefully will help others to preserve our national rail heritage.

The campaign to save the line has reached every part of the Kingdom, and a wide-ranging coalition, bringing together local authorities, consumer groups and political parties, has resulted. But, most importantly, local people have shown they want the line and need the line. That has provided the base for the wider community of the region to demonstrate clearly the role for the line in linking Yorkshire and the East Midlands with the West of Scotland -- in bringing together Nottingham, Sheffield, Leeds and Glasgow -- a real inter-city line! It is also an integral part of the local rail network in West Yorkshire. If the Settle to Carlisle were to close, would Keighley and Ilkley be next on British Rail's stealthy closure pattern?

And British Rail has confirmed it too needs the line -- to complement its other main line in time of trouble. Figures can be made to fit a case and the attempt to close the Settle to Carlisle line shows this all too clearly. If, like British Rail, you neglect your property, of course the maintenance bills will rise; if, like British Rail, you take away most of the services and retime the others for minimum convenience, of course passenger numbers will fall. But if the service is marketed and timed to meet passengers' needs, the line once again becomes vital and living. The case to retain the Settle to Carlisle line is all but made by the passengers -- they have made it one of British Rail's most successful services. The only question remaining -- is the closure procedure a conspiracy or just incompetence?

This isn't just a fight for a beautiful railway, it is a fight for the whole of our rail network and a fight to ensure the necessary new and continuing investment.

Wayne Jenkins,
Chairman,
Public Transport Committee,
West Yorkshire Metropolitan County Council.
December 1985.

PRESS CALL: West Yorkshire council leader Wayne Jenkins (left)
and Cumbria council chairman Eric Martlew at Garsdale station.
Picture -- Barry Wilkinson/Picture House

Introduction

SATURDAY December 17, 1983, will most likely go down in the
history books as the day of the Harrod's bombing. But 250 miles
north and a light year away from the bustle of Knightsbridge on
that tragic day, another event was making the news. Braving the
Pennine drizzle more than 1,000ft above sea level, a group of
senior local authority figures stood on the line at a lonely
railway station and delivered a Press conference. The backdrop
to this unlikely stage was the former London Midland & Scottish
Railway Duchess of Hamilton locomotive, the occasional belch of

steam from which swirled round at knee height and added to the surrealism of the scene.

"We give notice to British Rail that we don't like their methods and we don't like their stories," a defiant Wayne Jenkins, Chairman of West Yorkshire County Council's Public Transport Committee declared to assembled Press, TV and rather bemused steam train enthusiasts. "We want to replace rumour and fear with facts and reason," he continued. For this was the backlash: a group of local authorities putting their collective foot down and rushing to free the hapless damsel of public transport from Government captivity, tied to the rails before British Rail's onrushing closure express.

The place was Garsdale, formerly Hawes Junction, on the magnificent Settle to Carlisle line. The time was one month after British Rail had finally ended speculation and announced details of its plans to close the 72-mile route. The purpose of the "conference" was to launch a £34,000 independent assessment of the line to give the authorities opposing closure ammunition with which to challenge British Rail's own figures.

Those gathered to hear the speeches had arrived on board the Cumbrian Mountain Express, a round tour from King's Cross organised by the Steam Locomotive Operators Association. The train had taken on extra carriages at Leeds to house a most unusual mobile press conference. On board were officials and members from West Yorkshire and Cumbria county councils, representatives of the Yorkshire Dales National Park and the Countryside Commission, MPs, the 74-year-old County Constable of Cumbria Lord Inglewood, and British Rail officials -- in an issue as emotive as the killing of a railway few public figures want to risk being labelled "baddies" simply through not being there.

The trip had symbolic significance too, bringing together those with a professional or political interest in the future of the line with a train load of steam fanatics. Clearly any campaign to save the railway, should the independent survey uphold the wisdom of such a course, would need to enjoy the broadest possible support.

The initiative for the survey came from Cumbria and West

4

Yorkshire county councils but financial contributions were eventually forthcoming from virtually every local authority through or by whose territory the line passed. A prize convert to the cause was the traditionally low-spending vast shire county of North Yorkshire, not noted for its progressive attitude to public transport, but which nontheless contributed £2,000.

What had galvanised such ostensibly different authorities as metropolitan West Yorkshire and rural Cumbria into collective action was the threat to what is a significant part both of the railway network and of our national heritage. While the economic implications for Cumbria's Eden Valley and its emergent tourist industry were both worrying and obvious enough, it was less clear why West Yorkshire, whose boundary is 20 miles from the southern end of the line at Settle, should have taken so keen an interest in its future.

There were three reasons --

☐ The wish to preserve and develop the fastest and most direct strategic link between the conurbation and Scotland.

☐ The county's leading role in running the highly successful DalesRail excursions.

☐ The fear that closure of the Settle and Carlisle would seriously threaten the viability of the rump of the railway system remaining in West Yorkshire.

To understand why the issue arouses such passions and to give reasonable consideration to the plight of the Settle-Carlisle today demands an appreciation of just why the Midland Railway undertook more than 100 years ago to drive this remarkable line through some of England's wildest country. And so begins a history lesson....

Midland Compound No. 1000 and Leander No. 5690 at Aisgill
Summit, February 1983. Picture -- Ian Jopson

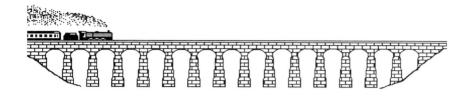

1. One man's dream

NESTLED amid a group of trees deep in the dale between the twin bulks of Ingleborough and Whernside, stands a tiny church. This was once called Waesdale, after the Anglo-Saxon word for pasture, but became Chapel-le-Dale after St. Leonard's chapel of ease was built early in the 17th century. The relatively lush shelter of the valley bottom which once inspired Turner and today provides a living for 200-odd people, is in marked contrast to the wild ruggedness of the fells above.

On the west wall inside St. Leonard's, a focal point for the nearest the dale comes to a centre of population, is fixed a tablet. It reads: "To the memory of those who through accidents lost their lives in constructing the railway works between Settle and Dent Head. This tablet was erected at the joint expense of their fellow workmen and the Midland Railway Company, 1869 to 1876." In the little churchyard a grassy bank beneath the trees gives no clue to the fact that more than a hundred years ago it was hurriedly consecrated to provide a shallow mass grave for as many victims of a smallpox epidemic. For the windswept, rainlashed landscape of heather, peat bog and bare limestone pavement which begins at Ribblehead just two miles updale -- in such contrast to Turner's idyllic Weathercote Cave -- was then a centre of considerably greater population.

The plague victims came from a hutted shanty town of wood and felt which housed 2,000 or more navvies and their families. Known originally and intriguingly as Batty Wife Hole or Batty Wife after a feature in the rock, the town became later Batty Green. Its people were engaged to build the two greatest structures on the Settle and Carlisle railway line, Ribblehead viaduct and Blea Moor tunnel. Today no sign remains of this or any other of the wild shanties -- Jericho, Salt Lake City, Battle-barrow-bank, and Sebastopol -- that sprang up along the 72-mile route.

But if this pinnacle of Victorian engineering achievement was expensive of human life, it was too of time and money. The building of the line was plagued by even wetter, colder weather than usual, adding to the turnover of labour which remained high despite the prospect of then good money at up to 10s for a 12-hour shift. The expenditure on candles alone for lighting the work in Blea Moor tunnel rose to £50 a month and as the original four years estimated for building the line stretched to nearer seven, so too did the cost: from £2.2m to almost £3.5m.

When the formal closure procedure for the line was begun late in 1983, some members of the British Rail hierarchy were almost gleefully describing the Settle and Carlisle as "the line which should never have been built", born out of a "fit of pique" on the part of Midland general manager James Allport who was frustrated at the problems which faced his company in trying to secure adequate routeing for its Anglo-Scottish traffic over other companies' metals. Indeed it can be argued quite plausibly from the evidence that the scheme was conceived as an enormous bluff by the Midland to try and achieve that aim by forcing the hand of its great rival, the London and North Western Railway.

The Settle and Carlisle was a product of what might be called the second period of railway mania in Britain, a mania fuelled in part at least by Parliamentary fear in the mid-19th century that any amalgamation between rival companies would lead inevitably to a much dreaded monopoly. Talks of amalgamation between the Midland, the London and North Western and the Great Northern railways in 1853 so alarmed Parliament that the prospect of approval for that or any future merger became very slim indeed. So the Derby-based Midland, sandwiched between rival routes north from London, was forced to expand to survive. With the completion of its extension to its own London terminal at St. Pancras, the company began to look towards increasing its share of Scottish traffic.

The Midland was able to run its trains as far north as the

village of Ingleton (at the western end of Chapel-le-Dale) via the Leeds and Bradford railway to Skipton and from there via the "little" North Western Railway which it also controlled. At Ingleton there was an end-on junction with a branch of the Lancaster and Carlisle section of the London North Western route: and therein lay the problem. The company's passengers were given such low priority by the LNWR that sometimes they even had to walk between the rival stations at Ingleton even though they were connected by a viaduct. The reward for such exercise would often be the sight of the rear of the departing "connection". Nor would the LNWR allow the through conveyance of Midland carriages for Edinburgh; nor stop its expresses at Tebay to connect with the trains from Ingleton. Mr Allport himself complained of having been unceremoniously conveyed to Tebay in a carriage attached to a train of coal trucks.

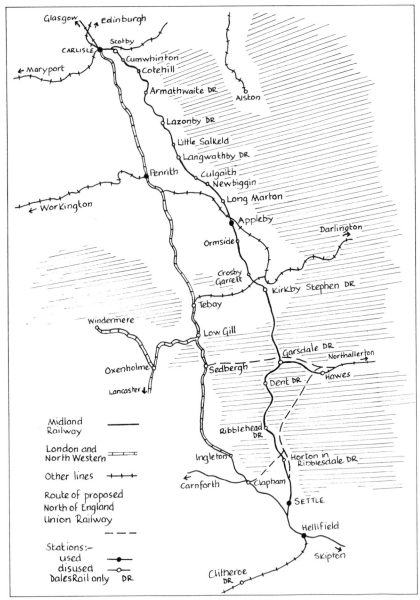

Map showing the Settle & Carlisle route in relation to existing lines and the proposed North of England Union Railway

The deadlock was such that Mr Allport and the company's chief engineer John Crossley decided to look again for their own route to Carlisle through territory which had previously been thought impossible by at least one railway engineer. An enabling Bill for a North of England Union Railway linking Hawes with Settle and Clapham on the little North-Western had already been passed by the Commons but before it reached the Lords the Midland intervened and the Bill was withdrawn to be reintroduced by the Midland in modified form. The original proposal envisaged a line down Wensleydale from Hawes to connect with the main network in the east and a branch from Hawes to the Lancaster and Carlisle branch at Sedbergh. The Midland plan still linked Settle and Hawes, but also provided a route north to Carlisle. It gained Parliamentary approval in 1866.

But the Midland's problems were not over: merger talk in Scotland between the Caledonian and the Glasgow and South Western railways threatened a bias in favour of the LNWR for traffic south of the border. So the Midland made its own approach to the G & SW with the result that the LNWR offered to reopen the question of Midland rights over its tracks -- if the Settle and Carlisle line was abandoned. Although the Midland at first declined, the building of the St. Pancras link and the Peak Forest line to Manchester had stretched its resources and, deciding on a policy of co-operation with the LNWR, the company sought permission to abandon the Settle-Carlisle plan. But by this time the Scottish companies and the Lancashire and Yorkshire Railway (which linked towns like Clitheroe and Blackburn with the little North Western at Hellifield, south of Settle) had become enthusiastic supporters of the new line and Parliament threw out the abandonment Bill.

If the whole process had indeed been merely a bluff, Mr Allport must have then been as sick as the proverbial parrot, for the Midland -- which had been staking out the proposed route somewhat half-heartedly -- found itself obliged to build an expensive railway it no longer wanted. The old North of England Union plan had envisaged following the convenient lie of the various dales and the Midland could no doubt at this point have satisfied Parliament by opting for a similar route along more modest lines than the direct Settle-Carlisle route proposed. The fact that Midland did not take this "easy way out" explains why the line is reckoned unique in the world as a **high speed** railway through "mountainous" terrain.

The company's aim remained to get its traffic to and from Scotland via the shortest and quickest route possible. The new railway was destined to be two miles longer than Settle Junction to Carlisle via Ingleton and Tebay, so the Midland engineers sought to overcome that disadvantage by building a line with no speed restrictions because of bends and with less severe gradients than the one-in-75 of the LNWR route over Shap Fell. The Settle-Carlisle is sometimes described as a "railway over the Pennines" -- this is not strictly correct as it both begins and ends west of the main watershed of the Backbone of England. Only at Garsdale Head, near its summit at Aisgill, does the line nudge the "spine" of the range at one of its lowest east-west crossings. On a train journey from Leeds to Carlisle the Pennines are actually crossed just east of Hellifield less than 500ft. above sea level, by means of the Aire gap.

So the Settle-Carlisle is not a trans-Pennine line but a railway driven through the hills. In his book Rails in the Fells, geographer David Jenkinson describes how the Midland's engineers chose "the best and, in fact, the only practicable way through these hills" consistent with providing a straight route with a maximum, or ruling, gradient of one-in-100. "It is doubtful if, even were the line being built today, the chosen route would be very different, fulfilling as it does all the functions one could reasonably expect of a modern rail line," he argues. That route involved a steady climb up the two north-south valleys of the Ribble and the Eden, with a ten-mile "mountain" section to be crossed between the valley heads. Here, remarkably, the line stayed almost level at 1,150ft. above sea level, clinging to the valley sides, soaring on lofty viaducts over tributary becks and plunging through the fells in deep tunnels. In all the line has 325 bridges, 21 viaducts and 14 tunnels: the workforce which built it peaked at 6,000 and made use of the latest technology, including vertical steam engines, steam lifts, drills and concrete.

Although built as a high speed trunk route, suggestions that the Settle-Carlisle made no concessions to meet any local traffic demands are misleading: in fact the start of the ascent from the Eden valley to Aisgill is delayed so the railway can properly serve the villages in the valley bottom and Appleby-in-Westmorland, with 2,384 people today the largest intermediate settlement on the line. The 40 miles between there and Settle is and was some of the most sparsely populated country in England, with only the market towns of Kirkby Stephen (1,540) and Hawes (1,111) boasting populations of more than 1,000 today.

Ribblehead viaduct under construction in about 1873. Part of the
Batty Green shanty town can just be seen in the background

The fact that the Midland's Kirkby Stephen station was built more than a mile from and some 350ft. above the town is usually cited as the most glaring example of how the line bypassed settlements in its quest for gentle curves and the easiest gradient. Yet there are numerous examples elsewhere of lines which went no nearer than a mile from the towns they were supposed to serve -- the similarly sized market town of Kirkby Lonsdale just off the route of the Lancaster and Carlisle's Ingleton branch is an obvious example. But to have served Hawes other than by the branch line which was built would have meant a major detour which would have slowed the route considerably.

Although there were few settlements of any consequence outside Ribblesdale and the Eden Valley, the Midland nontheless built 19 stations at fairly regular intervals along the line, some -- like Dent which is four miles from and more than 600ft. above the village of 590 people from which it takes its name -- being no mean distance from anywhere resembling a township. Despite this, detailed anlaysis of the available information, as carried out by Mr Jenkinson in his book, shows that the railway "made a substantial and valid contribution to local activity in the area", certainly until the advent of motor transport between the wars. Apart from anything else, the line opened up new markets for agricultural produce because it offered a speedy north-south link in an area where communications traditionally ran east-west along the dales.

When it opened, the line carried three through trains daily each way from St. Pancras to Edinburgh and Glasgow, with the fastest timing being ten-and-a-half hours to Edinburgh, compared with ten hours ten minutes by the more direct LNWR route or nine-and-a-half hours by the Great Northern. Mr Allport introduced the Pullman to Britain on the line and later, to the indignation of his competitors, abolished Second Class travel in favour of an upgraded Third Class. Four years after his retirement in 1880 he was knighted "for services to the poor traveller" -- a recognition which preceded by more than a decade the erection of the Chapel-le-Dale memorial to the builders of the Settle and Carlisle!

Through traffic on the line peaked just before the First World War when there were three daytime expresses each way between London and Glasgow and Edinburgh, and one between Liverpool and Manchester and the Scottish cities. One of the London trains conveyed a portion from Bristol and semi-fast services between Leeds and Carlisle carried through coaches from Lancashire and Bradford. Night trains linked London, Liverpool, Manchester and Bristol with Glasgow, Edinburgh and Aberdeen; and London with Stranraer via the direct line through Wigtownshire from Carlisle.

The service cuts caused by the First World War were followed by the 1923 grouping of the railway companies which saw the old rivals of the LNWR and the Midland become part of the London, Midland and Scottish Railway, marking the beginning of the decline of the Settle and Carlisle. Despite the LMS's concentration on the Shap route, there were again by the 1930s three daily return fast trains over the line, including the new Thames-Clyde and Thames-Forth expresses, the latter becoming the Waverley in 1957.

After the war, which had seen very heavy freight use of the Settle and Carlisle, there began the steady process of closures in the area which was to continue unabated until the 70s. The Ingleton branch and the Hawes-Northallerton section of the Wensleydale line closed to passengers in 1954. The demise of the remainder of the latter, connecting with the Settle-Carlisle at Garsdale, came five years later. The former North Eastern Railway from Kirkby Stephen to Tebay closed in 1960, and trains on the line east from Kirkby Stephen over Stainmore disappeared two years after that, as did passenger services on the Blackburn-Hellifield "feeder" to the Settle-Carlisle.

On the Settle-Carlisle itself, the first stations to close were in the Eden valley -- Scotby in 1942; Cotehill, Ormside and Crosby Garrett ten years later; and Cumwhinton in 1956. A rare item on the credit side in this period was the use of the line for the new Condor non-stop London-Glasgow night freights -- indeed the Settle and Carlisle remained an important cargo route until the eventual withdrawal of the last unbraked freights which could not be accommodated on the Shap route.

Tales of severe weather abound in books about the Settle and Carlisle. They range from the probable, such as the one about the icy Helm wind from the Pennines blowing the coal from the fireman's shovel, to the most improbable. The story about the railwayman being blown off a train on Ribblehead viaduct only to be sucked through an arch and back up on to the train at the other side stretches one's credulity. But it is worth mentioning the two harsh winters which succeeded in closing the Settle-Carlisle line: in 1947 it was beneath 12ft. of snow and ice for eight weeks from early February. Even a flamethrower failed to open a road, and when eventually it was possible to clear one track, the railway became a vital supply route for the remote dales. In 1962 the line was again blocked, this time for five days in January, an Edinburgh-London express being stranded at Dent until the railway was cleared sufficiently to extract the last three coaches back the way they had come.

The Beeching report brought the first generalised threat to passenger services on the line after the British Railways Board announced its intention to withdraw the local stopping service at 12 stations between Hellifield and Carlisle. But with the benevolent concern for the welfare of people and that willingness to place narrowly-based financial considerations second typical of a Government on its assumption of power, Tom Fraser, the Minister of Transport in the new Labour administration refused permission for the closure in November 1964. The grounds were that undue hardship would result, this being the yardstick for assessing closure plans by the transport users' consultative committees under the 1962 Transport Act.

Freight services had nonetheless been withdrawn from the stations served only by local trains in the course of 1964 and they were then reduced to unstaffed halts in an effort to cut costs. But the reprieve was shortlived as the service fell the wrong side of the line drawn according to the "Cooper Brothers' formula" -- the new test introduced at the behest of the Ministry of Transport for assessing the "viability" of rural rail services. In simple terms, the thinking behind this was that services such as the stopping trains on the Settle and Carlisle should bear a proportion of the overheads involved in maintaining the line as a whole.

Now the nonsense of this apparently reasonable proposition only becomes evident when you start to talk about actually withdrawing services -- because shutting a local service whose contribution to overheads is considered insufficient does precisely nothing to reduce those overheads. In fact the nett result is that the overheads fall even more heavily on the remaining services. Nonsense or no, this became the altar on which many lines and services were axed in the late 60s and early 70s.

In the case of the Settle and Carlisle, the British Railways

Board was able to argue that the cost of running the local service was some £102,000 a year, against which fares income from an "official" 43 regular passengers was just £9,000. This figure was so far removed from the actual (marginal) cost of running the diesel multiple units on the line that the passengers could have been given free Champagne breakfasts on every trip within the costs quoted. As Colin Speakman -- who was destined later to play a prominent role in the revival of services on the line -- observed in a letter to the Yorkshire Post in January 1969: "This is a new strategy of rail closure -- exaggerate the costs to deaden the protests." Working on figures from the Beeching report, he put the true cost at a maximum of less than half the British Rail figure. The closure proposal -- surfacing in the now traditional manner of an early Christmas present at a time calculated to minimise the effectiveness of any opposition -- could hardly be described as having come out of the blue. The noises emanating from the railways board over the past few years had been such that Malcolm Barker, writing in the Yorkshire Evening Post in March 1967, had been able to make an authoritative suggestion that "the end is not far away" for the Settle and Carlisle, of which all that would remain would be stubs at either end as far as Horton-in-Ribblesdale and Appleby.

The "regular users" figure concealed the fact that some stations were well used in summer by visitors to the Dales, many of whom would presumably have travelled on connecting services on other parts of the rail network. George Ellison, the chairman of Dent parish council, summed up the dilemma: "We are seeing the Dales die and we want to do all we can to keep them alive. The railway does more than give us a way out -- it gives other people a way in." The council noted in a letter to the North-West TUCC that there could be 30 or 40 people on trains to and from Dent bound for the youth hostel near the remote station. Ramblers were duly urged to object to the closure plan by Jack Smith, secretary of the West Riding branch of the Railway Travel and Correspondence Society, which in January 1969 ran a special excursion on the Settle and Carlisle which was also the last train to run on the Waverley line before it was closed.

In the case of the Waverley it had proved impossible for a powerful lobby of local authorities, industrialists and individuals to prevent the complete loss of a 98-mile trunk route which, while passing through wild and remote country, served sizeable towns whose population totalled about 100,000 -- five times that served by the Settle-Carlisle. The chances of success for the 60 individuals, 23 local authorities and other bodies, and 12 youth hostellers who objected to the loss of twice daily Carlisle-Skipton and the daily Garsdale-Skipton and Appleby-Carlisle services were clearly slim.

In April 1969 the TUCC reported that the loss of local services would cause severe hardship to those who relied on them to travel to work, college, hospital, doctors, dentists, chemists and for all the other numerous social reasons that people, quite reasonably, use railways. The committee found itself unable to suggest any means of reducing this hardship.

A year after the withdrawal of the local service was proposed, the people of Dent and the other communities served were given another Christmas present, when transport minister Richard Marsh advised British Rail that -- while he appreciated some travellers would face considerable increases in their journey times -- their numbers were so small that the retention of the trains could not be justified. The last local trains ran in May 1970 and the stations at Horton, Ribblehead, Dent, Garsdale, Kirkby Stephen, Long Marton, Newbiggin, Culgaith, Langwathby, Little Salkeld, Lazonby and Kirkoswald, and Armathwaite were closed. This left Settle and Appleby the only intermediate stations on the line, as they are today.

By August, in response to claims that remaining services on the line were being deliberately slowed down, British Rail stated that 100mph grading was no longer commercially viable. In May 1981, BR was sufficiently bold to state: "The eventual aim is that the line will be severed at a point near Horton-in-Ribblesdale and near Kirkby Stephen and will be abandoned between those two points."

In 1977 the loss of the St. Pancras to Carlisle and Glasgow services paradoxically brought some improvement as the Nottingham-Glasgow trains which replaced them took the direct electrified route north of Carlisle rather than the detour via Dumfries and Kilmarnock. The six-hour timing for the run was, unusually, half an hour faster than that achieved by the Midland in its heyday.

The following year British Rail had a change of heart and added the Settle-Carlisle to lines on which occasional steam-hauled excursions would be permitted.

And that was roughly the state of play when talks of a rematch in the old closure game began to circulate again in the early 80s. In the meantime, however, something quite remarkable had been going on on the Settle-Carlisle -- something British Rail said could never work but whose success would later provide thousands of objections to, and a compelling argument against, the closure of the line.

Plan of the 1985
DalesRail operation
showing bus
connections

CARLISLE
Armathwaite
Lazonby
Langwathby
Roman Wall
Middleton in
    Teesdale
Appleby
Barnard Castle
Glenridding
Tebay
Kirkby Stephen
Keld
Reeth
Cautley
Hawes
Leyburn
Sedbergh
Garsdale
Dent
YORKSHIRE
DALES
Barbon
Ribblehead

**DALESRAIL
AND BUS
CONNECTIONS**
● ● ●**Runs only
on specific
dates**

Horton in Ribblesdale
Settle
Hellifield

Skipton
Keighley
Shipley
Clitheroe
Bingley
PRESTON
Bamber Bridge
Blackburn
now with connections from other B.R. stations
BRADFORD
LEEDS

20

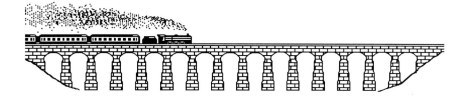

2. Who dares wins

ASTROLOGERS would say it was written in the stars; a palmist would doubtless find some kink in the lifeline to explain it; some would put it down to fate or divine intervention; and others would feel there was little point in looking for particular reasons why a combination of circumstances should suddenly change the course of a person's life.

Sometimes such monumental changes for the individual have a broader effect on people or society at large. It would be pompous to suggest Colin Speakman's unplanned exchange of a life at the blackboard for a desk in a national park office was to leisure transport in Britain what the jailing of Jean Genet was to 20th century French literature. Colin would be the first to admit that it was a happy intervention of many different circumstances which helped to make the DalesRail ramblers' charter trains such a dramatic success, despite the doom-laden prophecies of critics. And yet it seems fair to say that those critics were so outspoken that without someone of Colin's commitment to the idea and his conviction that integrated rail/bus access to a national park could work, DalesRail might never have happened. And if DalesRail hadn't happened, then -- as this book will explain -- the closure of the Settle and Carlisle might have been a very much easier task for British Rail to achieve.

No-one who has met Colin would disagree that he is one of life's organisers -- our meeting at his Ilkley home was sandwiched between work and organising a lecture on Turner in the Yorkshire Dales. At the end of our talk, while his wife tried to nail him to the kitchen table to eat some tea, he busily organised a cargo of Yorkshire Dales Society material for me to convey to a far-flung member. Back in 1970 he was a 29-year-old English teacher in Leeds. Born beneath the red rather than the white rose, like so many others he fell in love with the Yorkshire Dales while at Leeds University and chose to stay east of the Pennines. At that time his organisational bent was satisfied within the West Riding Ramblers Association, for which he became access officer, then transport officer and finally Area Secretary.

"In those days I was a weekend rambler, with no car," he recalled. In the late 60s it was quite easy to be a weekend rambler without a car as British Rail ran ramblers' specials from Leeds to places like the North York Moors, the Peak District and the Yorkshire Dales. The Dales excursion ran on the Settle and Carlisle line and "there was a great tradition in this region of trains, countryside and walking". "Everybody used to say that the best one of the lot was the Settle-Carlisle excursion," said Colin.

In addition to the excursions, lobbying by the ramblers had persuaded British Rail to introduce cheap day tickets on stopping trains to intermediate stations on the Settle-Carlisle line. More successful lobbying followed in 1969 when BR was persuaded to lift its previous year's embargo on running specials. "The crunch came in May 1970 with the end of stopping services -- that effectively cut off a third of the Yorkshire Dales National Park for people without cars," said Colin, whose family found themselves deprived of their principal leisure activity. "I was a militant anti-car person but we gave up and bought our first car -- not to get round town but to get round the countryside."

But it was another four years before the germ of DalesRail was sown -- in the shelter of a dry stone wall on a rainy Pennine Easter Monday. Colin and fellow ramblers Jim McDermid, Fred Andrews and Jeff Grange were taking a rest while on a gritstone walk from Rochdale to Marsden. They were indulging in that time-honoured pastime of bemoaning the stupidity of British Rail when it was suggested by one of them that the Ramblers Association should put its money where its mouth was and charter a train over the Settle-Carlisle. Getting BR permission to stop at the closed stations as a "one-off" proved, contrary to expectations, rather easier than subsequently persuading the West Riding Ramblers Association to risk putting a relatively small amount of money up front to charter a train. "We had a hell of a meeting and it went finally by a very small majority in our favour," said Colin.

"We went ahead and advertised it as well as we could and there was an avalanche -- we started off hoping we might get 200 people. We ended up with a ten-coach train loaded to the 'gunwales'." So when the train actually ran in late summer 1974 not only were cost-conscious members of the Ramblers Association silenced, but 500 walkers enjoyed a grand day out and the people of Garsdale station were able to do something they hadn't done for more than four years as they came out of their former railway cottage homes and waved to passengers on a departing train.

Colin Speakman

At around the same time, local government in England and Wales was undergoing its biggest shake-up for decades as county boundaries were redrawn, new counties created and old ones abolished or swallowed up by their larger neighbours. As part of the 1972 Local Government Act, the Yorkshire Dales National Park ceased to be simply a joint planning committee of the North and West Riding county councils and became instead a fully fledged National Park Committee of North Yorkshire County Council.

It also included representatives from Cumbria and members appointed by the Secretary of State to represent the special "national" interests of ramblers, conservationists and other amenity groups. Colin Speakman was one of the appointed members.

At the same time, a threat from British Rail which had been looming in the wings suddenly moved centre stage: it was claimed that if the Settle-Carlisle was to provide a satisfactory diversionary route for the West Coast main line, the platform edges of its disused stations would have to be demolished to allow sufficient clearance for the new Mark Three coaches. This would obviously have put paid to the idea of ever repeating the successful ramblers' special -- and yet BR's claims seemed to be quite inconsistent. It was never satisfactorily explained, for example, just precisely what it was which necessitated a different amount of clearance at a disused station compared with one which remained in use. It was tempting to believe that this was a cynical attempt to pre-empt any successful ramblers' service on the Settle-Carlisle lest it should eventually prejudice attempts to close the line. BR engineers were told as much by national park members at a stormy meeting at Settle in the winter of 1974.

Yet out of that working party meeting, comprising representatives of the park, British Rail, Cumbria county council, Eden district council and the United and Ribble bus companies, came a decision to restore five stations and operate an experimental charter service with connecting buses from Garsdale station to Hawes and Sedbergh. Colin -- freshly inspired by a trip to Switzerland where he had been impressed by an integrated transport system which ensured anybody could get from the tiniest village to anwhere in the country in a day -- presented a paper to the park committee proposing a fully-fledged Dales rail service. With the park throwing its weight behind the principle, Colin resigned his member's seat to apply for the newly created post of Field Services Officer to which he was appointed in January 1975.

He now attributes that rapid progress towards an ideal to the heady idealistic days early in the life of the park when there was a real belief in the ability to make things happen. "DalesRail could not have happened with the old authority," he said. "The crisis of the stations and the success of the ramblers' train all happened just as the new authority was coming into being." Armed with all the optimism of the park committee, Colin and the Assistant National Park Officer, George Hallas, went to Leeds to talk to British Rail about the cost of restoring the stations. "They told us 'we in this room represent 140 years of railway experience and we think this is a total waste of time'. But we eventually persuaded BR to restore stations to a standard fit for 'occasional use' for a total of £5,000 instead of £15,000 each."

Colin attributes the progress made to the then Preston Division Passenger Manager, David Harrison, who he believes saw in DalesRail an opportunity to win for British Rail a cash injection, albeit a very small one, from local authorities and thereby set a useful precedent. The next major hurdle was presented by the Railways Inspectorate whose safety requirements for an advertised DalesRail service were somewhat higher than for the occasional excursion stopping at the occasional disused station. With the first scheduled train just three weeks away and all the publicity material ready to go out, there was still no approval from the inspectorate. A question in the House from Keighley MP Bob Cryer finally elicited the necessary information and the first DalesRail ran from Leeds, Bradford, Shipley, Bingley, Keighley and Skipton to the national park stations plus Kirkby Stephen and Appleby on the first weekend in May 1975. There were two trains on the Saturday and one on the Sunday, when the connecting buses were extended to run into Swaledale. Guided walks led by volunteers were arranged from various stations and bus-stops.

The legal niceties included indemnifying British Rail against possible injury to passengers, and providing voluntary wardens to look after passengers at the stations. At Ribblehead -- where the private owner had woken one morning to see bulldozers demolishing the down platform and waiting room to make way for new sidings at the British Rail ballast quarry -- special arrangements had to be made and new access provided to the remaining platform.

Despite the short period left for publicising the venture, the first DalesRail was well used and the loss of £127 rather than the £372 which had been budgeted for was judged by the Yorkshire Post to be "beyond the revivalists' wildest expectations". It was due entirely to the cost of the connecting buses and concessionary fares which were enjoyed mainly by Dales families using the southbound trains. Dales park chairman Keith Lockyer declared: "There are 18,000 people living in the park area and they receive seven and a half million visitors every year, most of them in cars. We want to cut down the number of cars coming into the park and give the locals a link with the West Riding shopping centres."

Things went from good to better as the June and July trains ran with standing room only and by the end of the six-day experiment 3,370 people had used the service and there was support for an extended trial aided by a £4,000 three-year grant from the Countryside Commission. Extensions to DalesRail that autumn included a "long weekend" service and trains from Preston over the freight only line between Blackburn and Hellifield. It was a time of innovation, fired by a certain idealism: "We actually used the local government and the National Parks Act as a way of making things happen," recalls Colin. Thus when it was pointed out the national park had no power to renovate stations outside its boundaries in the Eden valley, it simply gave the money to Eden District Council to do the work instead. And when in December 1975 it was realised it could not legally run a shoppers' special for dalesfolk to Leeds, the park ran a guided walk at Garsdale for six West Yorkshire people to comply with the letter of the act.

By the end of the year 5,497 passengers had travelled on DalesRail, generating an operating surplus of £165, rather than the loss of £2,000 which had been budgeted for. The most popular of the reopened stations were Kirkby Stephen, the destination for 967 travellers and the departure point for 461, and Garsdale, where 919 alighted from and 557 boarded trains. Dent was also popular as a destination for 747 DalesRailers.

Colin was enjoying "magnificent" support from Coun. Lockyer and National Park Officer Richard Harvey and gained the benefit of an assistant, Andrew McCullagh, who was appointed in November 1975, thanks to Countryside Commission funding. He had every reason to be optimistic and 1976 saw the extension of services to and from Carlisle and three reopened stations at Armathwaite, Langwathby and Lazonby, with a linking bus service to the Lake District and guided walks organised by the park authority there.

AWAYDAY: Guided walk leader and Yorkshire Dales National Park Committee member Laurie Fallows helps ramblers off a DalesRail train at Garsdale (above), while others take the bus to Sedbergh or Wensleydale. Pictures -- Colin Speakman.

The following year was one of consolidation, with a 12 per cent reduction in passengers to 5,363 due largely to a policy of operating shorter trains filled to capacity rather than risk over-ordering stock from British Rail. September 1977 also saw an experimental DalesRail on what remained of the Wensleydale line, running between Newcastle, Durham and Darlington and Bedale, Leyburn and Redmire. The three year DalesRail experiment was pronounced a success and the park resolved to continue it on a regular basis, despite the end of the Countryside Commission grant. Not only did the scheme enable access to the park by people without cars, but it also offered the chance to manage the number of visitors in particular locations through the guided walks which were enjoyed by some 62 per cent of the Sunday rail users in 1977. DalesRail had made a name for itself and was commended by the British Tourist Authority.

But Colin's expectations of a growing Dales park transport department organising minibus services, rail links and so on were shattered that year when Andrew was unexpectedly moved to planning duties against the background of a subtle shift of opinion in the park hierarchy away from recreation towards conservation. The feeling was that care should be taken not to attract too many visitors through schemes such as DalesRail. "I needed half a guy's time to make DalesRail work," said Colin. "They didn't consider DalesRail important enough -- I was the only person with any seniority who was in favour." Believing the shift in attitude posed a threat to the very existence of the service, Colin set up the Friends of DalesRail, whose secretary Les Watson -- who was reading for an MSc in ·rural transport at Leeds University -- took on responsibility for organising stewarding on the trains.

The chance to make good the loss of his marketing man came in June 1977 when Colin met Robin Ward, the Director General of West Yorkshire Passenger Transport Executive, at a "fun day" to mark the revamping of Keighley station. He persuaded Mr Ward that as DalesRail was using stock which during the week ran PTE services, the PTE should turn its considerable resources to selling DalesRail tickets and promoting the service. Against the background of a promise from the Countryside Commission of

28

help in promoting recreational transport generally, the PTE took on the marketing of DalesRail, and went on to take over the chartering of trains from British Rail, taking advantage of its ability to negotiate a better price than the national park could. Under the PTE regulations laid down by the Government, it was possible for DalesRail trains to be, effectively, PTE trains as far as Settle, 20 miles beyond the West Yorkshire boundary. In 1978 the PTE rechartered the trains to the national park committee, but this arrangement was "forgotten" in subsequent years, with the result that the PTE was now effectively running the service.

One of the beauties of the PTE involvement was that DalesRail passengers were able to start their journeys from any station on the PTE network -- at a time when the executive was faced with having to make unpopular service cuts, here was a service which could raise the PTE in the public's estimation.

With the future of DalesRail secured by a broader footing outside the park, Colin found increasingly that the old flexible interpretation of park rules was being eroded and he faced new instructions such as that guided walks and connecting bus services should no longer cross the park boundary.

The reopening of Clitheroe station on the Blackburn-Hellifield link in 1978 brought Lancashire county council and Ribble Valley council (which had funded the Clitheroe scheme at minimum cost, thanks to British Rail flexibility) into the DalesRail steering committee and -- with Cumbria, Eden district, the national park and the United and Ribble bus companies -- there were now eight authorities co-operating in providing the service. "There has still, to my knowledge, never been any other kind of co-operative organisation in public transport like that since," said Colin.

Eventually, the Countryside Commission kept its promise to the PTE and set up the three-year Wayfarer recreational transport project. Finding the national park increasingly unable to provide the working environment he wanted for running DalesRail, Colin chose -- at some cost to himself -- to trade his salaried post in the Dales for a three-year contract to organise the Wayfarer project at West Yorkshire. "I had been in charge of DalesRail at the national park -- I then turned up the following year at the same meeting sitting on the PTE benches representing the 'big boy'."

At the time of writing, DalesRail had become an established feature on the Settle-Carlisle, with around 6,000 passengers annually, through-ticketing facilities on British Rail and PTE services, and connecting buses to Teesdale, Lonsdale, the Lakes, Hadrian's Wall and the high Pennines. Colin, for his part, was County Tourism Officer for West Yorkshire -- a job due to disappear with the metropolitan authority in April 1986. But given his growing reputation in the field of leisure transport, that end could well mark the start of new beginnings for the former English teacher....

3. Beeching is dead - long live Lord Beeching

"HE was in the headlines long after ceasing to be British Rail chairman in 1965. His memory reverberates among mourners of quiet country railway stations as well as among students of brisk post-war attempts to modernise Britain." Thus ran the obituary of a journalist's son from East Grinstead in The Guardian on March 25, 1985.

The death of Lord Beeching at 71 merited some 29 column centimetres, a measure of the notoriety achieved by the man whose name became synonymous with the word "axe". The report continued: "Lord Beeching's attempt, as architect of the 1963 Beeching plan, was one of the first and most drastic, and he was always bitter that his 'scientific, free enterprise technique for running a state service' was not allowed to go further."

Dr Richard Beeching was a brilliant physicist and technical director for ICI who had been brought in by the Tory government to perform drastic surgery on the railway system, for which he was paid what was dubbed the "Himalayan" salary of £24,000. He was to the railways in the 60s what Ian MacGregor became to steel and coal in the 80s. The first phase of his plan demanded the closure of 5,000 out of 17,800 route miles and 2,300 of the 4,709 stations, a process which continued into its second phase until the 1967 Labour Government announced a stabilised network of 11,000 miles.

Although Dr Beeching described his axeman's reputation as "an injustice I shall suffer in history", his was the single most swingeing assault on the railways in their history. But his report was only one of many learned documents that have helped

31

shape today's residual rail network. The continuing report-chop-report-chop process which has created the situation where rail management can glibly propose lopping the 72 miles of the Settle-Carlisle off the national network has its origins half, or even a whole century ago.

If the 20th has become the century of the roads lobby, then equally the 19th was that of the railways. At a time when Parliament reigned rather more supreme than today, it was estimated that up to 150 MPs represented the "railway interest". Parliament sanctioned the building of all the railways by authorising the acquisition of the necessary land, but there was no attempt by Government to do so in a way that helped produce an overall efficient national network. Indeed the reverse was true -- Parliament's pathological terror of monopoly mentioned in chapter one permitted the proliferation of wasteful duplication. Routes were paralleled -- the Midland, Great Northern and Great Central railways running within a few miles of each other north of Nottingham is a classic example. Cities, towns and even villages where a single main station would have sufficed acquired two, or often more. Different companies adopted different standards, making any ultimate integration more difficult. Even today the tight tolerances on bridges and other structures on the old Furness Railway make use of the Cumbrian coast line very difficult as an alternative diversionary route to the Settle-Carlisle, without major expenditure. Physical links where rival networks crossed were often complex or non-existent. The exceptions were the North-Eastern Railway, which built up a regional monopoly in North-East England with consequent savings in efficiency, as did the Great Western in the West Country.

The position -- worsened by the problems facing managements in learning to cope with the new phenomena of widely dispersed workforce and assets -- is summed up by Kerry Hamilton and Stephen Potter in their book, Losing Track: "It was a massive overprovision which turned the railways from a potentially very prosperous industry into one where profit levels were relatively low. When, half a century later, the problems of this railway development process came home to roost and Lloyd George's government had to deal with the mess, Lloyd George's verdict was that it had been 'a gigantic waste'."

By the turn of the century, although nearly one in eight of the working population was employed by the railways, the position of many companies was insecure and their numbers declined rapidly as they were absorbed by larger ones. But the imminent threat of war in 1912 prompted the Government to impose on the railways a 20th century national management in the shape of the Railway Executive Committee, whose subsequent operations served to highlight the inefficiencies of the old-style competition. The 1919 establishment of the Ministry of Transport granted wide powers to rationalise, even nationalise, the railways -- nationalisation had not then acquired today's party political overtones and was supported by Lloyd George and Winston Churchill. Even earlier -- in 1844 -- the Gladstone Act had given the Government an option to acquire post-1844 railway companies after 1865.

But the railways resisted nationalisation to sink back into their 19th century ways and it was only in the face of looming crisis that the 1921 Railway Act led to the compromise grouping of the railways into four large companies, the London and North-Eastern, the London Midland and Scottish, the Southern and the Great Western. But the Act failed to reform any of the old 19th century powers aimed at regulating inter-company competition and protecting customers from the powers of monopoly transport. So as road haulage began to grow, the railways found themselves obliged by statute (under the "common carrier" principle) to carry small loads of freight at low revenue which the road carriers could refuse to handle. The combined assault of the roads and the deepening depression saw the railways facing falling traffic, to which their response was an attempt to reduce staff numbers and downgrade clerical posts as they became vacant. The collapse of the 1926 General Strike weakened the railway unions and wage cuts and unemployment followed more easily.

Most historians agree that, faced with an accelerating loss of trade to the roads, the railway managements failed to come up with the sort of aggressive marketing and operating policies which might have helped them retain or expand their traffic. They did not seek to charge higher rates for their captive heavy freight customers like the coal industry, nor did they reduce prices for conveying goods which were most vulnerable to seizure by road competition. The temptation was there, it is argued, simply to blame the injustice of the common carrier obligation and do nothing. On the plus side, the LMS did take the initiative in introducing the container to rail freight, for which premium rates **were** charged.

Professor Philip Bagwell, the National Union of Railwaymen's official historian, argues that the railways' meagre financial returns led directly to their failure to invest adequately in modernisation between the wars, at a time when those in other countries were doing so. While gross investment between 1920 and 1938 was £283m., this was only about two thirds of the amount required merely to cover depreciation. The Weir Committee report on electrification in 1931 argued that to secure the full economic advantage of such a scheme most of the country's main line system should be converted -- possibly with state subsidy -- to electric traction, at a total cost including power stations of £341m. over 15 to 20 years.

The publication of the report coincided with another severe drop in traffic and all that came of it were token schemes such as the Sheffield-Manchester Woodhead route (now closed). Steam, after all, was a proven technology and Britain still had an abundance of suitable coal. Describing it as "one of the great missed opportunites of the 1930s", Prof. Bagwell comments in The Transport Revolution from 1970: "In any case many leading railwaymen were more interested in improving the performance of the steam locomotive than in making exhaustive inquiry into the economics of electric traction." The notable exception was the Southern, whose network was rather more suburban in nature than that of the other railways.

There **were** areas in which the railways did invest, however -- road and air transport. But rather than using such investment to set up "feeders" to their own services, the companies were more interested simply in "spoiling" the plans of road and air operators. The Royal Commission on Transport commented in

1931 that the railway companies' principal response to the road threat appeared to be to "get on the road" themselves. "Insofar as this policy makes for the better co-ordination of rail and road services we welcome it. On the general principle of the policy, however, we cannot refrain from expressing a feeling of doubt whether it is wise for the companies to expend large capital sums for the purpose of establishing services which may be in direct competition with their business as railways. We feel that possibly such capital would be better applied to the electrification of their suburban lines."

On the question of air routes, the views of the former LMS Chief Secretary, P.E. Garbutt, on the company's Railway Air Services venture are quoted in Michael R. Bonavia's book, Railway Policy between the Wars: "The basic purpose in setting up Railway Air Services and developing internal air services, railway owned, in the United Kingdom was to suppress possible competition....They were mainly concerned with getting in on routes, establishing themselves and then operating a holding exercise, a restraining exercise, to stop anybody else from getting in and building up a substantial air traffic."

The notion that transport operations produced benefits to their users and the areas they served which were not necessarily of benefit to the operators themselves began to be appreciated in the 30s. The seeds of a nationalised transport network were sown by the first minority Labour Government in 1929 and London Transport came into public ownership in 1933.

But it took another strength-sapping war in which the railways were flogged to the brink of exhaustion before nationalisation became a reality with the setting up by Labour in 1945 of the National Transport Board to co-ordinate state-owned rail, road, water and air services. The 1947 Transport Act established the British Transport Commission to which the railways and other transport undertakings were transfered on January 1, 1948. The Act offered the potential of a fully integrated national transport system: unfortunately the five executives under the commission -- rail, London Transport, docks and inland waterways, hotels and road transport -- tended to have what Hamilton and Potter call "an independence of outlook which positively hindered the transport integration objectives of the Commission".

That wasn't the only problem: the wartime traffic boom had arguably inflated the price paid by the Government to the operators for their railways, on which there was a massive legacy of repairs to be carried out. By 1951, when the Tories were returned to power, the only obvious success of the commission in moving towards transport minister Herbert Morrison's dream of an integrated system had been in building up the road haulage side. The Churchill Government's first act was to sell off the road haulage executive with its new lorries at bargain prices, often to the very operators who had received compensation for their battered old fleets only three years previously. The role of the British Transport Commission as an integrating body was ended by the 1953 Transport Act which denied railways the role of operating the "middle leg" of door-to-door freight services. While the private enterprise road hauliers had been given a spanking new asset to make money with, the railways were still languishing in their pre-war torpor, making do with worn-out, obsolete equipment which -- as already described -- was effectively a legacy from the last century. The Government had split them into regions based largely on the old pre-war companies and which were responsible directly to the British Transport Commission.

But many sectors of private industry were still dependent on an efficient railway and so the new BTC chairman, Sir Brian Robertson, was given a brief to update the system. The commission's plan for the modernisation and re-equipment of the railways was launched with no fewer than three press conferences -- one for news reporters, one for leader writers and one for financial editors -- on January 21, 1955. It was a bold scheme born out of six months' intensive work and envisaged spending £1,200m. over 15 years to achieve "a transformation of virtually all the forms of service now offered by British Railways". There would be fast, clean, regular, frequent services in urban areas and faster, punctual inter-city trains. Services on other routes would be made "reasonably economic" or transferred to road. Improvements to the freight service would "attract to the railway a due proportion of the full-load merchandise traffic which would otherwise pass by road". The scheme's main elements were --

☐ £210m.-worth of track and control improvements, including coloured light signals and removal of bends and other speed restrictions on trunk routes to obtain 100mph working.

☐ A £345m. programme to replace steam engines with diesel and electric traction, including the electrification of the main lines from London to Liverpool, Manchester, Leeds and (possibly) York.

☐ Replacement of steam-hauled passenger stock with diesel or electric multiple units at a cost of £285m.

☐ Modernisation of freight-handling services at a cost of £365m.

The commission envisaged an annual return of at least £85m. on this investment, half of which, it pointed out, would be required in any case for normal maintenance work. But by 1959, with many works started, the Government was getting cold feet. The only part of the programme -- whose cost had risen, partly owing to inflation, to £1,500m. -- which was pursued to completion was the replacement of steam. The reason lay in the advent of mass car ownership which, as Hamilton and Potter put it "represented the 'you never had it so good' way of life". The 50s saw the coming of age of the "roads lobby", as the Society of Motor Manufacturers and Traders joined forces with the Road Haulage Association to form the British Road Federation. At the same time, the shift from traditional heavy industry to new industries like car building saw the Transport and General Workers Union in the ascendant at the expense of the railway, mining and other unions.

The rise of the car was reflected and fostered in Government until the appointment of Ernest Marples as Minister of Transport in 1959 marked the effective final transformation of the Ministry of Transport into the "Ministry of Roads". Marples owned the major road construction company Marples Ridgeway but sidestepped the problems of having such a clear vested interest by the simple expedient of passing his shareholding to his wife. Thus began a noble Conservative tradition of giving to those with an interest in the roads, positions of power over the railways -- a tradition which it seems was still thriving with the appointment of the Serpell committee in 1982.

The 1955 Robertson report had made no fundamental criticism of the railways, but Marples was soon able to demote still further their political status when he appointed an advisory group under Sir Ivan Stedeford to examine the running of the BTC. The Stedeford report called for an end to railway management's "public service" mentality and said they should be run as a profit-making business. The BTC was duly abolished by the 1962 Transport Act and a member of the Stedeford group, Dr Richard Beeching, was appointed the first chairman of the British Railways Board. Beeching may have disliked the axeman's label, but seen in the context of the politics of the time it becomes clear that if Marples was the picador who disabled the railways bull, then Beeching was the matador appointed to administer the fatal blow.

The method of administration was to be by means of a document euphemistically called The Reshaping of British Railways which appeared in 1963. If Beeching had been a brilliant physicist, this document -- the Beeching Report -- exposed his shortcomings as a transport econonomist and statistician, certainly by today's academic standards. At best Beeching's assumptions were naive: at worst they were a crude device to justify railway closures to the ultimate benefit of the roads lobby.

As Hamilton and Potter put it: "The Beeching Report was not just a shopping list of railway closures, but did provide an analysis of the role of the railways in Britain. However, the criteria and methods adopted to evaluate the role of the railways meant that major closures were a foregone conclusion.

"For example, the relationship between road and rail was considered only to the extent that Beeching felt free to suggest that unprofitable rail services could be transferred to road. The possible effects on roads and whether it would require more to be spent on roads to accommodate such traffic than would be spent on the railways was not examined. He concentrated attention on the cost of retaining railways and gave no consideration to the costs and consequences associated with developing the road network."

Beeching's studies led him to conclude that one third of the country's route mileage (5,900 miles) was generating just one per cent of the passenger and freight ton miles. Half the network carried just four per cent of the total passenger mileage and five per cent of the freight mileage, and generated annual revenue of £20m. towards costs of £40m. The other half of the network, by contrast, was generating revenue six times its route costs, argued Dr Beeching. These bald figures led him to conclude that the lightly loaded lines should close, and as soon as possible. He seems to have been particularly deaf to any serious consideration of ways of making lines more economic through investment or improved productivity, and instead offered token consideration to ideas such as fares cuts, reduced services, station closures and rail buses to replace diesel units. This cursory examination led him to assert that the idea that such services could be retained as an economic alternative to buses was "really not so". The Beeching closure yardstick was that any service which did not generate sufficient revenue to cover its "direct costs" should go -- that remains the narrow test of "viability" which applies even today: all that has changed is the accounting trick whereby the Government chooses from time to time exactly how far along the scale the stick should be placed.

Beeching made two bold assumptions: firstly, that all former rail passengers would readily transfer to the replacement bus services. In this he chose to ignore all questions of speed, comfort and reliability (particularly in bad weather), and all those marginal sociological and psychological factors which make rail an acceptable form of public transport for many and buses an unacceptable one. Mayer Hillman and Anne Whalley present figures which amply illustrate this point in their study, The Social Consequences of Rail Closure. They found that only in socio-economic groups D and E did more than half the former rail passengers transfer to the replacement buses. In other groups the figure was much lower. Among car owners who had formerly used the railways, the transfer to buses after closure was very small indeed.

Soon many of the bus services were losing more money than the trains they replaced -- and they did not even have to cover their own "track" costs! Worse news for people in rural areas particularly was that, unlike the rail services, they could be withdrawn without resort to any legal process as was required in the case of railway closures.

Beeching's second bold assumption, made on the basis of just one week's survey work, was that the railways would retain 95 per cent of their traffic after the closures. This assertion was based on ludicrously optimistic assumptions about the retention of feeder traffic after the routes on which it was generated had closed. One of the examples he quoted was the direct Hull to York line via Beverley which bears some comparison with the Leeds-Carlisle route today, in that it linked two cities via a fairly thinly populated rural area. The service on this line on Beeching's own figures actually more than covered its operating costs, but allowing for terminal and track costs showed an annual shortfall of £60,400. Of the £90,400 direct earnings, Beeching expected to lose £64,790. But out of the £37,680 spent by passengers on the line on tickets for journeys beyond Hull and York (contributory revenue), Beeching expected to retain all but £4,900. Closure, he said would yield a nett annual benefit of £81,110. Experience quickly showed Beeching's assumptions about contributory revenue to be false and by 1969 passenger journeys on British Railways had slumped to 805 million from 1,025 million in 1961, and freight by 13 per cent over a similar period during which 4,000 route miles of railway had closed. There were developments Beeching could not have predicted, such as slower economic growth and the decline of the coal and steel industries -- but another factor, the growth of car ownership and use, was in part at least a direct consequence of his actions. In simple terms, Beeching had failed -- or not wanted -- to appreciate that if you cut the roots and branches from a tree the trunk will wither.

The railway unions' attempts to resist Beeching through the TUC appeared thwarted by the increasingly powerful Transport and General Workers Union and alternative plans which would have yielded similar savings through improved efficiency were rejected by the railway management. In all, Beeching's massive closure programme had no appreciable impact on the railways' need for revenue support. Meanwhile, Lord Stonham had identified the nett subsidy to the roads as £600m. a year -- four times that given to the railways. But the Beeching closures gave a fillip to road building by adding to congestion and increasing the clamour for new investment to reduce both delay and the rising toll of accidents. The doctor's reward for this failed social experiment was elevation to the House of Lords.

The whole question of how the economic model is made to favour road investment is dealt with in more detail in Chapter Ten, but it is worth first quoting in full Beeching's passing reference to the broader question of the comparative social cost-benefit of rail and road: "It might pay to run railways at a loss in order to prevent the incidence of an even greater cost which would arise elsewhere if the railways were closed," said his report. "Such other costs may be deemed to arise from congestion, provision of parking space, injury and death, additional road building, or a number of other causes.

"It is not **thought** [*author's emphasis*] that any of the firm proposals put forward in this Report would be altered by the introduction of new factors for the purpose of judging overall social benefit. Only in the case of suburban services around some of the larger cities is there clear likelihood that a purely commerical decision within the existing framework of judgment would conflict with a decision based upon total social benefit. Therefore, in those instances, no firm proposals have been made but attention has been drawn to the necessity for study and decision."

Pictured overleaf by Ian Jopson, Sir Nigel Gresley, No. 4498, approaches Aisgill summit, Mallerstang, from the north in June 1985. Note the kestrel waiting for small animals to be disturbed at the track side.

Funnily enough, someone else was -- on a brief from Marples -- doing another study which, had the "Ministry of Roads" chosen to put the two side by side, had important implications for the Beeching Report and vice versa. Colin Buchanan's Traffic in Towns report was already pointing to even greater costs than feared due to congestion, accidents and pollution caused by road traffic. But never the twain shall meet...

The closure programme continued more or less unabated through governments of both main persuasions, certainly as far as concerns the lower density routes with which this book is most concerned (the benefits conferred by the 1968 Transport Act, insofar as they applied to the railways were important only in the main conurbations).

The test of viability facing branch lines and rural stopping services would go on to see various changes, as already indicated. Now, with the branches well pruned, there arose the possibility of some paring of the trunk itself. The British Railways Board report, The Development of the Major Railway Trunk Routes, which appeared in 1965 represented the application of the Beeching branch line philosophy to the main lines. This report sought to present a "critical examination" of the trunk routes "to establish how the through route system can best be developed to match the future pattern of rail traffic demand". Its aim was to rid the railways of the effects of the wasteful duplication caused by the 19th century's competitive building.

It identified major railway traffic centres and the flows between them and then looked at the number of different routes between which that traffic was shared. Out of 7,500 miles of trunk route, 3,700 miles were duplicated, 700 were triplicated and 700 quadruplicated. The report suggested that this network was under-utilised to the extent of some 60 per cent. Based on similar assumptions about national economic growth to Beeching, the report predicted a gradual progression over 20 years towards its recommended route pattern. Many of its suggestions have never been implemented, but the document provides a useful insight into the assumptions which were being made about the railways.

These were typified by the apparent view that trunk routes

led from A to Z and the fact that traffic might be generated at intermediate stops from B to Y was given relatively little consideration. There was a further implicit assumption that traffic between A and B could always be retained even if forced to pass via C, where C represented the third corner of a triangle. Thus the report believed that all the Anglo-Scottish traffic could be accommodated on the West Coast route, with the Newcastle to Edinburgh traffic being routed via Carlisle. By and large the trunk routes have survived the 20 years since the report, with notable exceptions like the Waverley line and the Great Central. Curiously, the Woodhead route from Sheffield to Manchester which was selected as the preferred southern trans-Pennine option became the one which was actually closed.

If as much energy as has gone into producing reports about how to dismantle the railway system in Britain had been put into making it more efficient, we might today have a viable modern national network. The Serpell Report, commissioned in 1982 at a cost estimated at well over £500,000, is probably the most spectacular example to date and for that reason alone deserves some consideration. Making the same questionable assumptions about bus substitution and the retention of contributory revenue as had been made by Beeching 20 years earlier, Sir David Serpell and his committee set about producing a series of options tailored to varying levels of Government support.

The committee's conclusions were spectacular in their outrageousness -- Option A for a "commercially viable railway" envisaged an 84 per cent network cut and no lines in Scotland north of Edinburgh and Glasgow and no East Coast route north of Newcastle. Option B reinstated those lines where the "resource cost" of withdrawing the service would be greater than retaining it. The various C options envisaged differing levels of support, while Option D reinstated services to towns with a population of 25,000 or more. The high investment Option H was so superficial as scarcely to merit mention.

The approach showed conspicuous inconsistencies. On the one hand, the strategically important Newcastle to Carlisle line would be axed under most options. On the other, Serpell saw a future for the northern Scottish routes **and** for the run-down Settle-Carlisle. The explanation was quite simple -- routes like Inverness to Kyle of Lochalsh had had their costs pared to the bone and had been made more efficient through investment. Newcastle-Carlisle had 26 manned signal boxes and so its costs were artificially inflated through lack of investment.

But Serpell's faults ran even deeper. The report's commissioning was a political solution to the differences evident between the British Rail chairman Sir Peter Parker and the Tory Government. It was presented by the Government as the review which BR had asked for. But if Sir Peter had agreed to a review, it is hard to imagine he would have wished to see conclusions such as those drawn by the Serpell Committee. The one consolation was that the Serpell report eventually became widely discredited and an embarrassing exercise the Government was glad to forget in the course of the 1983 General Election. It implied that rail safety standards might be lowered towards those pertaining on the roads. There even remains some question as to whether the consultants remembered to include freight revenues in their calculations (Hansard, Janaury 20, 1983).

The Serpell report can be seen as just another shallow and sorry manifestation of the power of the roads lobby and it is this aspect of it which perhaps deserves more attention than its clear methodological shortcomings. The committee was chaired by Sir David Serpell, a member of the British Railways Board. Its members included Leslie Bond, James Butler and Alfred Goldstein. Mr Goldstein was a senior partner in R. Travers Morgan and Partners and Mr Butler a partner in Peat, Marwick, Mitchell and Co., both firms with an obvious interest in road transport. More surprisingly, both firms benefitted directly by being commissioned to carry out work worth several hundred thousand pounds for the Serpell Committee on which their own partners were sitting.

The question was raised as a point of order in the Commons by the then Labour MP for Keighley, Bob Cryer, who suggested that money had been paid to the firms in contravention of the Government chief accountant's rules (Hansard January 20, 1983).

Mr Cryer's Lewisham West Labour colleague Christopher Price called for an adjournment of the House to discuss "the clear breach of the Government chief accountant's guidelines in the appointment of R. Travers Morgan and Peat, Marwick, Mitchell & Co. as consultants to the Serpell committee". These guidelines stated: "A candidate firm will be ruled out, without detailed consideration, if.....there is a clash, or potential clash, of interests that would result from its appointment." Mr Price continued: "Our principal responsibility in the House is to ensure that Government moneys are spent properly and without leaving the Minister or his civil servants open to accusations of sharp practice, jobs for the boys, corruption or anything like that." The debate ended with the Speaker ruling that if the question was to be pursued it should be done "in some other way".

On February 16 Mr Cryer asked an oral question of the Transport Secretary David Howell: "Is it not curious that, although the Secretary of State always rabbits on about competition, these consultants were chosen without any competitive tendering whatsoever, contrary to the general rules of conduct applying to such business?" Mr Howell cited the urgency with which the consultants' submissions were required as bringing this unusual practice within the rules: "The consultants were chosen because they could give prompt backing to those selected to help with the review." In answer to a question from Mr Robert Hughes, he continued: "The rules for the employment of consultants make it clear that in exceptional circumstances an approach to a single firm may be made." The Tory "Falklands" landslide removed some of those Labour members who had been pursuing the Serpell appointments most vigorously and like so many other issues it has become largely forgotten.

The report itself, it has been suggested, was to some extent guided towards its extreme position by Mr Goldstein who subsequently -- having made his mark -- withdrew from joining in the main report to publish his own minority view in an appendix. Discredited or not, the Serpell report must be considered to have had influence on the course of the railway finances debate if only because any cuts suggested now will appear preferable to the most extreme suggestions contained in it.

Today the security or otherwise of railway lines is governed largely by a complicated accounting procedure which seeks to allocate costs to various lines and areas of activity, or "sectors". The five British Rail sectors are: London and South-East, Provincial, InterCity, Parcels and Freight. The Government already requires the freight sector to operate without requiring subsidy. It therefore follows that BR accounts procedures will always seek to "load" the infrastructure costs -- track, signalling and so on -- of its freight operations on to the other sectors where possible. The "prime user" principle determines the allocation of costs between sectors and, in the metropolitan counties, local rail services supported by the Passenger Transport Executives under Section 20 of the Transport Act.

This fact helps explain why the InterCity sector -- which the Government says must make a £36m. profit by 1989 -- might have wished to remove its services from the Settle-Carlisle on which it was prime user (see Chapter Four). With most freight traffic similarly removed, this left the Settle-Carlisle effectively part of the loss-making Provincial Sector, supported by Public Service Obligation grant. It is in this way that Government policy is effectively pushing BR towards a Serpell-style route-cutting solution.

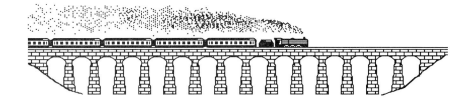

4. A comedy of errors

ON August 9, 1984, was written probably the most bizarre act in British Rail's Settle and Carlisle tragi-farce. This was the day when a record third attempt was made to publish notice of the intention to close the line. Attempt number one was launched in the guise of the by now traditional Christmas treat for passengers on December 15, 1983, but the procedure was abandoned the following April as it foundered on a legal reef. Attempt number two followed in May, 1984, and -- with the simultaneous reissue of closure notices for the Goole to Gilberdyke service on the Doncaster to Hull line -- marked the first known occasion on which a closure procedure had had to be restarted.

Attempt number three was most remarkable for the fact that it related to just three miles of track with no stations. And because there were no stations, the closure notices had to be posted at the nearest sizeable settlement -- namely Hawes, to where trains had last run back in 1959! But the first lines to the script of this comedy of errors were really written some years previously.

The inspiration, some might say the scapegoat, for the drama appeared in the majestic form of Ribblehead viaduct. Those acquainted with the manner in which British Rail apparently does these things detected the first tentative tinklings of the alarm bell in 1981. These came in the form of a remarkable "exclusive" in the April issue of Steam World, which said BR was considering building a new viaduct at a cost of £4.5m. and refusal of funds for the project could lead to the closure of the line. An article in the Yorkshire Post of May 19 that year, by the

New Civil Engineer's northern editor, David Haywood, said the viaduct's condition was terminal. Quoting British Rail's divisional civil engineer Alan King, Mr Haywood wrote that BR had spent £600,000 on repairs to Ribblehead over the previous ten years but had ended up with a structure in worse condition than when they started. The work had included strengthening the pier corners with concrete and replacing the brick lining beneath two of the arches. But the failure of the waterproof membrane on the structure's deck had allowed the piers to fill with water which then washed the mortar out from the inside. This in turn had the effect of leaving the limestone blocks of which the viaduct was built supported upon the different sized grains of mortar which remained, thus subjecting them to uneven loadings. The 290 million-year-old limestone had reached the end of its life and a replacement viaduct was needed, the report concluded bluntly.

British Rail's repeated and strenuous denials that there was any connection between the decision to "go public" on Ribblehead and the various other decisions affecting the fate of the Settle-Carlisle around this time remains difficult to swallow. Some of those other decisions were quite public, such as the announced intention to reroute the Nottingham-Glasgow service via the West Coast main line and Manchester, thereby avoiding both Leeds and the Settle-Carlisle. It was maintained that this decision -- to take effect from May 1982 -- was a purely commercial one on the part of BR's InterCity sector which saw the revised route as likely to generate more intermediate traffic. The Yorkshire Area Transport Users' Consultative Committee was sceptical about BR's assurance that this would not prejudice the future of the Settle-Carlisle "especially as the proposed alternative services for Yorkshire passengers are ill-drafted and inadequate".

The committee noted that these Yorkshire passengers represented more than 50 per cent of those using the existing service -- for the first time in more than 100 years there would be no through trains from Leeds to either Glasgow or Nottingham. The subject provoked more complaints to the committee in 1981 than did any other. If the InterCity managers had identified a greater potential for a service via Manchester they were also prepared to forego known traffic via Leeds and further worsen an already poor service between Leeds and Sheffield. Typical journey times between Leeds and Nottingham were extended from less than two to almost three hours, leaving the door wide open to coach operators to pick up the already proven traffic.

Rather less public were the behind-the-scenes machinations from which it is clear that a decision to close the line was taken in principle well before the announcement of the Nottingham-Glasgow diversion. A confidential BR document in August 1981 linked the condition of Ribblehead viaduct with the broader issue of whether the line was needed at all and predicted closure by 1984. The then fairly considerable freight traffic and the Nottingham-Glasgow trains should all be diverted via the West Coast route, it said, and a "residual" Leeds-Carlisle service introduced as a legal stopgap. It was anticipated the transport users' committees' considerations would be concluded by May 1984. Through freight traffic was indeed diverted -- often by ridiculously circuitous routes -- and local quarry traffic was forced on to narrow Dales roads as BR cited a lack of available locomotives to convey it. The line was reduced to daytime only working.

So clandestine were the discussions leading to this policy, it seems, that BR chairman Sir Peter Parker was able to write to Barbara Castle MEP that July: "Once again let me stress that our recognition of the changing role of the Settle-Carlisle line does not imply that we are anxious to ensure its closure. At present we have no plans in that direction." In October Sir Peter was again putting pen to paper, this time in a letter to the Leeds Tory MP Sir Donald Kaberry: "I feel it worthwhile to emphasise that while we certainly have no desire, or indeed plans, to close the line at present we do have very real problems with investment." These "problems" included Ribblehead and other viaducts and tunnels which were in imminent need of major remedial work. Sir Peter hedged his bets even less in a letter to Bradforth North Labour MP Ben Ford: "I would ask you to accept my assurances that we have no desire, or at this time plans, to close the Settle-Carlisle line." One must assume that the BR chairman, then, was unaware of the plan contained in the August document, all but the last stage of which had by this time been put into effect.

With BR now saying that no decision would be taken pending the findings of an independent consultant's report on Ribblehead, West Yorkshire County Council voiced concern at the increased burden the diversion of the Nottingham-Glasgow service would place on the Leeds and Bradford to Skipton link.

The damaging uncertainties continued into 1982 and in March, at a private briefing, MPs were told by BR officials at Preston that closure was planned but that this information was not for public release. The Yorkshire TUCC noted in its annual report: "Throughout the year the shadow of impending closure loomed over the Settle and Carlisle route, described by British Rail as 'the most spectacular main line in England'. By the beginning of October informed opinion was of the view that a Section 54 Notice giving prior warning of closure proposals would be published by January 1983; something which the London Midland region did not seek to deny to the committee at the time."

But in November the Skipton and Ripon Tory MP John Watson claimed the British Railways Board had over-ruled the London Midland Region plans for imminent closure, possibly because of the likely political row. The London Midland general manager wrote in reply to letters from the TUCC: "There is no change in the situation regarding this line -- we are still collating information." The TUCC noted that the line had probably been granted a stay of execution rather than a reprieve and commented that if BR wished to seek closure it "should have initiated closure proceedings prior to the re-routeing of the Nottingham-Glasgow service away from the line, thus absolving themselves of any charge of 'closure by stealth'".

Against a background of refusal to make simple improvements to the Leeds-Carlisle service -- typified by the arrival in Leeds of the train from Carlisle two minutes after the departure of the Kings's Cross trains with which it had connected comfortably in the previous year's timetable -- BR maintained this "no decision" stance until August 1983 when the intention to publish a closure notice was announced.

This news did, if nothing else, mean that BR's cards were at last on the table and everyone knew what they were up against. BR's past insistence that re-routeing the Nottingham-Glasgow trains would not prejudice the future of the Settle-Carlisle line for which it said it had no closure plans, were described charitably by the Yorkshire TUCC as exhibiting a "lack of candour". Bob Cryer, ousted as Labour MP for Keighley in the 1983 "Falklands" General Election, was rather blunter and blamed a Government-inspired "hush" policy which had kept BR's true intentions secret until after the election and the subsequent by-election in William Whitelaw's Penrith and Borders seat.

It is worth noting that in the meantime the old excuse of left and right hand synchronisation difficulties was still trotted out regularly by BR. When Mr Cryer described the missed connection at Leeds to me as "a deliberate attempt at sabotage", Peter Maynard at the London Midland's St. Pancras press office replied: "If the Eastern Region have recast their InterCity 125 services I can't explain that from a London Midland point of view, because I don't write their timetables." He added: "We are not deliberately setting out to prevent people from making connections."

Between August and the commencement in November and December of the closure procedure in accordance with the 1962 Transport Act, the financial basis of BR's case began to emerge. It was claimed closure would save an annual operating loss of £600,000 and £9.75m in maintenance over the next five years. Yorkshire Post journalist Alan Whitehouse delved a little deeper into the figures. BR's projected 1983 running costs of £722,000 compared with an actual cost in 1982 of just £304,000. That staggering 137.5 per cent increase was made up as follows:

☐ **Diesel fuel** -- up from £59,000 to £147,000 at a time when the true increase was under 12 per cent.

☐ **Short-term maintenance of locos** -- up from £37,000 to an astonishing £158,000.

☐ **Train crew costs** -- up from £11,000 to £27,000, whereas the national pay award was equivalent to just 4.5 per cent.

☐ **Maintenance** -- up from £48,000 to £153,000.

☐ **Depreciation** -- now £11,000 instead of £3,000, whereas the only actual change was the addition of two coaches to trains.

The cause of these inflated figures appeared to be the sudden allocation to the line's accounts of 2.5 locos and 14 coaches compared with 0.6 locos and 4.4 coaches in 1982. It seems that with the re-routeing of the Nottingham-Glasgow trains which only travelled over the line for a fairly small proportion of their total journey, BR was now able to attribute all the costs of the two loco-hauled daily trains to the Settle-Carlisle alone. It was also suggested that some maintenance work, such as the relining of Blea Moor tunnel, had been accelerated so as artificially to load maintenance costs on the line. Questioned as to the confusing nature of these figures, BR told Mr Whitehouse: "To discuss individual sets of figures would serve only to confuse the issue." Mr Whitehouse rejects subsequent BR attempts to explain the sudden massive increase in costs by claiming one set of figures related to a half and the other to a full year. My own interpretation of the leaked document on which Mr Whitehouse based his piece is that BR's version just won't wash.

Meanwhile the disincentives to travel continued: Paul Holden, station master at Appleby, had to run his own campaign to extend the Super Saver fares available at stations on the West Coast route to those on the Settle-Carlisle. Who was going to travel from Appleby to London for £52 when they could go from Penrith on the main line for just £17? Receipts at the station, it need hardly be said, had already slumped alarmingly from the last week of the Nottingham-Glasgow through train compared with the first week of the new service.

So the closure express had finally come out of its siding and was gathering momentum -- but in the meantime the opposition had also been marshalling its resources. In June 1981, prompted by the uncertainty fuelled by the Nottingham-Glasgow diversion plans, the Friends of the Settle-Carlisle Line Association held its inaugural meeting at Settle town hall at the instigation of DalesRail enthusiast Graham Nuttall from Burnley. David Burton, a Rolls Royce aero-engine worker from Colne, was elected chairman.

Although the Friends quickly built a substantial membership there were grave doubts among more seasoned lobbyists as to the association's ability to mount the sort of informed political campaign necessary to counter British Rail's advantage. Images of a meeting of the Bradford Railway Circle early in 1983 spring vividly to mind -- I had gone to interview Mr Burton for a piece I was writing for the New Statesman. A group of wide-eyed railway buffs sat huddled in a draughty church hall and gazed lovingly at a nostalgic slide show of mighty steam engines plying the Settle and Carlisle. At the back of the hall Mr Burton set up a trestle table from which he sold items of railway memorabilia: the message that seemed to come across was "let's hope they don't close the line or we won't be able to take pictures of steam-hauled excursions at Ribblehead".

A few months and one closure announcement later and the Friends, with about £1,000 in the bank, were thrust to the forefront of the fight to save the line -- could they handle it? In March that year the Railway Development Society -- the national rail pressure group -- had launched its own campaign at a meeting in Leeds. The society's North-West chairman Richard Watts had been in close touch with the Friends but was concerned that the association was ill-prepared for the imminent announcement of closure proceedings.

"I had tried several times to gear up the Friends as an effective body," said Richard, a history teacher from Preston. "It was pretty obvious we had to get them into a campaigning frame of mind -- to make them a little more politically aware." To that end he had produced for the Friends a leaflet setting out the events which suggested BR was engaged in "closure by stealth", and this had become the association's principal campaign document. But the leaflet failed to catalyse any independent action by the Friends -- attempts to politicise the association seemed doomed to failure.

At the same time, Richard was in contact with John Whitelegg and Peter Horton at Lancaster, who ran Cumbria and North Lancashire Transport 2000 as a vigorous campaigning group. An exploratory meeting of representatives of all three bodies revealed a wide divergence of views between the way the RDS and Transport 2000 saw the Settle-Carlisle campaign developing and what the Friends were prepared to do. "It was obvious it was necessary to have a new body that had the appearance of uniformity," said Richard. And so out of that was born the tri-partite Settle-Carlisle Joint Action Committee, an at times uneasy alliance between the Friends, who had strength in numbers, and the RDS and Transport 2000 who had campaigning and political experience.

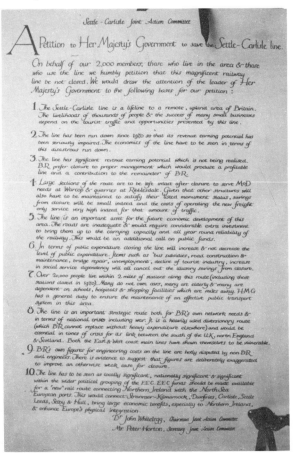

The Joint Action Committee's petition, drawn by Alan Ward --
Picture by Paul Kellis.

With Dr Whitelegg in the chair, the new alliance quickly adopted a high profile campaign. It accused Transport Secretary Nicholas Ridley of misleading the Commons over the Settle-Carlisle closure plans so as to protect the Under-Secretary David Mitchell and avoid further embarrassment over the discredited Serpell report; it called for a full Public Inquiry into the closure rather than the limited format of TUCC hearings; it prodded and probed at the BR hierarchy teasing out the odd leak here, the odd mistruth there. Trains and homes throughout the North were subjected to a leaflet blitz. It all added up to a style which did not come naturally to the then Friends' leadership -- but if the new alliance needed them, then equally the Friends needed that alliance too, or face eclipse in the public eye.

At first the members of the joint action committee met only briefly at the various public meetings held along the length of the line. "That was obviously very unsatisfactory," said Richard. "It was obvious that more and more of the work was apparently being done by John and Peter and we began to wonder what the Friends were up to." The salvation of the alliance proved to be the formation of a limited company, master-minded by Peter Horton, which formalised the relationship between the three independent groups in August 1984. John Whitelegg became company chairman, the tireless Peter Horton its secretary. The other board members were Richard Watts and -- from the Friends -- Philippa Simpson and Brian Sutcliffe, their new chairman. The committee opened an office in Lancaster and set out on a major fund-raising initiative, primed by a £2,500 grant from the Rail Union Federation. At the suggestion of Des Wilson -- the Freedom of Information campaigner who addressed a meeting at Settle town hall -- the campaign base was widened to include all the other interest groups involved in the Settle-Carlisle fight. This broad base was formalised at the committee's December 1985 annual meeting when some 18 groups, ranging from chambers of trade to the Youth Hostels Association acquired the right to board membership.

Peter Horton went on, through the board of Transport 2000, to establish the national Standing Conference on Rail Closures -- the first body with the aim of co-ordinating opposition to rail closure plans nationwide (whose number in process is well into double figures at the time of writing).

On the NUR's special protest train are, from left -- Peter
Horton and John Whitelegg of the Joint Action Committee, Roy
Hattersley and NUR Secretary Jimmy Knapp.

The anti-closure bandwagon was attracting support from an increasingly wide range of people from landed gentry to Labour -- the shadow transport secretary Gwynneth Dunwoody presented a lengthy protest petition to the Government and the party's deputy leader Roy Hattersley pinned Labour's colours to the campaign mast when he travelled on the National Union of Railwaymen's special over the line in February 1984. The action committee claimed to be able to reach the parts their peers couldn't, with senior civil servants telephoning the committee to check discrepancies between its claims and those of BR. "They are coming to us because we have demonstrated there is more to this closure proposal than the minister is aware of," said Dr

Whitelegg in the summer of 1984. "It's very rare that a dialogue has opened up between central Government and a group of 'unwashed scruffy campaigners'."

But for all the self-denigration, Dr Whitelegg draws upon a not inconsiderable professional and academic experience in transport and the workings of Government which has enabled him to represent the Settle-Carlisle case on an equal footing with BR and the Department of Transport. Graduating from the University of Wales at Aberystwyth in 1970, he completed a research project on industry in the Potteries to gain his PhD. From 1973-76 he directed a Department of Transport-funded project at Cardiff into the movement of heavy freight, thereby gaining an insight into the workings of the department on his weekly visits to the Marsham Street headquarters. The purpose of the research was to predict demand for road and rail transport of iron, steel and coal. One of the principal findings was that political decisions on the location of industries had exacerbated transport problems. "It was typical Government-funded research," said Dr Whitelegg. "We made all sorts of recommendations and nothing was done with the information."

He then worked as Transport and Development Officer for the Western Isles Council on Benbecula in the Outer Hebrides "doing what local authorities in England employ 50 or 60 people to do". It was a challenging and enjoyable position he never really intended to give up, but -- because of the virtual non-existence of a freehold property market in the Hebrides at that time -- his family faced the prospect of homelessness, against which his employers could offer only a caravan.

Never seriously believing homelessness would become a reality, he began applying for jobs in universities as a safeguard. But with the Western Isles council unable to improve on the caravan offer, he ended up taking a lectureship in Lancaster University's geography department after just 18 months in the Hebrides. Since it is reasonably safe to assume he would never have become involved in the Settle-Carlisle campaign had he remained there, the Western Isles council may well have a lot to answer for in the eyes of British Rail!

Dr Whitelegg and his wife Midge are people who believe in practising the philosophies they preach -- they find living in Lancaster compatible with not owning a car and educate their four children, aged seven to 13, at home.

Dr Whitelegg sees the action committee's independence as vital in enabling it to present a "more agressive" case against closure at the TUCC hearings than, say, local authorities which may be constrained by political protocol. But the local authorities, meanwhile, were very far from idle. Once a closure proposal appeared to be on the cards, a joint steering committee of officers and members of West Yorkshire, Cumbria and Lancashire county councils was established. This led, upon British Rail's formal announcement, to the commissioning of the £34,000 PEIDA report, described in the introduction to this book. This move typified a remarkable degree of co-operation between authorities of differing sizes, interests and political complexions. While the Steering Committee comprised two members each from West Yorkshire, Cumbria and Lancashire, financial contributions also came from Bradford, Calderdale, Carlisle, Craven, Eden, Leeds, Pendle, and Richmondshire districts; Settle town council; the Countryside Commission, the English Tourist Board, the Yorkshire Dales National Park and British Rail. The last named may sound curious, but those who rode on the Cumbrian Mountain Express Press special on December 17, 1983 will remember the confidence of BR's man Ron Cotton that the report would substantiate its claims about the line's financial position. "We are convinced of the facts of the case from a business point of view," he said.

Later chapters of this book will deal with the findings of the PEIDA report and give some insight into the behind-the-scenes lobbying carried out by county officers at Westminster and elsewhere.

Ron Cotton had an unenviable task that winter's day, enjoying all the popularity of a thunder storm at a Test Match. "Actually, I'm human," he told those assembled at Garsdale Station to cries of "rubbish". In the first appointment of its kind, Mr Cotton had been made Project Manager for the Settle-Carlisle line -- BR Newspeak, if you like, for the man charged with closing it. In fact the brief given to this former divisional passenger manager at Liverpool was a wide one encompassing not merely the smooth running of the closure process but also marketing the line in such a way in the meantime as to maximise revenue. The choice of Ron Cotton for the job had raised a few eyebrows within BR -- many thought he would have been just the man to promote the line as going rather than a half-gone concern.

Faced with the threat of long-distance coach service deregulation in 1980, Mr Cotton had pioneered the Saver ticket on the Liverpool-London service and -- in marked contrast to the direst predictions of those who thought it would only eat into BR's existing market -- saw revenue on the route rise more than £20m. in the first year. Soon the Saver was copied in other London Midland divisions and it eventually became the "standard" cut-price ticket throughout BR. But far from being rewarded for his initiative with a move to higher things, Mr Cotton -- a 52-year-old father-of-four -- found himself with arguably the most unenviable position in the London Midland. Like so many large organisations, BR moves in mysterious ways....

**Ron Cotton -- Pic
Barry Wilkinson/Picture
House**

Back on the Press train, Mr Cotton's Manchester-based public relations colleague John Searson pulled few punches when he told me: "The huge disparity between revenue, no matter how well extended to cover all the markets we think might exist, and the very high outlay to maintain the bridges and tunnels is so great that whilst the study may shorten the gap a bit, it will never shorten it to such an extent that the viability of the line can measurably improve." He concluded bullishly: "As we see it, the line has not got a cat in hell's chance of ever achieving viability." He went on to tell how through "better management of mishaps" on the West Coast main line, BR would be able to avoid having to use the Settle-Carlisle as a diversionary route.

The wisdom of that remark was soon called into question by a succession of diversions over the line, most notably in June 1984 when it was used on at least four separate occasions because of track and overhead wire failures on the West Coast route. Mr Cotton, for his part, was enjoying mixed success: his marketing flair brought such a boom in passengers -- despite the inconvenient timings and antiquity of the rolling stock -- that he was forced to schedule an extra daily train that summer after angry would-be travellers were left standing on the platform at Appleby. So hastily had this service been inserted into the timetable that even BR's own Travelcentres were unaware of its existence the day it started running, a deficiency the Joint Action Committee set about remedying by producing its own promotional leaflet in the guise of an official British Rail one.

But if Mr Cotton was fareing over-well on the marketing side of his brief, the closure aspect was going rather badly. In January 1984 a letter from Roger Smith, vice-chairman of the Greater Manchester Transport Action Group, prompted the Yorkshire TUCC to look closely at the detail of Section 56 of the Transport Act under which the closure procedure was being carried out. What it found was to have wide repercussions not only on British Rail plans to close the Settle-Carlisle but on other closure proceedings in hand. The TUCC found a major discrepancy between the British Rail notice of closure published under Clause Seven of Section 56 of the Act and the grounds for objection as set out in Clause Eight. Although the format of the closure notice was the same as that which had been in use for 20 years, it seems nobody had noticed that whereas the BR notice stated "any users of the rail service it is proposed to discontinue" could lodge an objection, the text in the Act actually said "any user of any service affected" was entitled to do so. The committee immediately drew BR's attention to the discrepancy -- the initial response was an insistence from BR that the only valid objectors to closure were those travelling over the section of line it was proposed to close. Under the possible threat of legal action from the Joint Action Committee, BR gave way and in April announced that both the Settle-Carlisle and Goole-Gilberdyke closure notices would be reissued to "broaden the scope for making objections".

The effects of this climb-down by BR were twofold: in the first instance it settled the row which had been brewing over the question of DalesRail users who had already objected to the closure even though the BR notice limited the scope for objection to those who travelled on regular BR services to and from Settle and Appleby. In the second instance it cleared the way for a whole new field of objections from DalesRail passengers using the reopened stations on both the Settle-Carlisle and the Blackburn-Hellifield link. On May 17 the notices were reissued and the closure procedure was started again from scratch, with the result that during the six weeks allowed for them to be lodged, the number of objections received by the Yorkshire TUCC alone rose by 5,931 to 7,467.

One Sunday early in August I received a tip-off that BR, fearing a red light further down the legal track, was about to reissue its Section 56 notices again. This if-at-first-you-don't-succeed approach to railway closure seemed hard to believe and demanded disturbing Ron Cotton at home: the tip-off, as the introduction to this chapter will have indicated, proved well founded. BR had overlooked the fact that the line strayed briefly, near its summit at Aisgill, into the Richmondshire district of North Yorkshire which fell within the area of the North-East TUCC rather than that of the Yorkshire TUCC. Mr Cotton said: "We decided to readvertise in the North-East to make sure there is absolutely no cause for criticism and to block all possible loopholes. I don't think it puts us back at all -- the only fact as I see it is it gives six more weeks for people to get objections in."

But despite Mr Cotton's attempts to put a brave face on things, the new setback attracted the anticipated ridicule and disbelief. The North-East Area TUCC chairman James Briggs refused to believe it at all, saying the question had already been discussed and the need for reference to his committee discounted because there were no stations involved. Then, having also disrupted Mr

Cotton's Sunday and been given the same information, he said: "It's amazing to me if BR have given way on this as they have already given way on one issue." His opposite number in Yorkshire, James Towler, was less incredulous: "It's really quite extraordinary and bizarre, but I have been about sufficiently long not to be surprised or astonished at anything involving BR." The Joint Action Committee immediately planned to make the most of the extension by means of a leafleting blitz throughout the North-East and Dr Whitelegg said: "It's absolutely astounding -- it proves the whole thing has been messed up from the word go." And he observed: "I think BR are basically incompetent and I think with more time and resources they could have been tripped up on practically any railway closure."

Although the BR notice, published in Darlington newspapers, invited objections to be sent only to the North-East TUCC, some 7,430 were sent to the Yorkshire TUCC over the next six weeks, compared with just 69 to the North-East TUCC. The Yorkshire committee found itself obliged to remind BR that objections could, under the Act, be lodged with any of the three TUCCs and advised BR that its views on the validity or otherwise of objections was irrelevant and "could be mistaken as an attempt to interfere" in the committee's business.

The legal rows were not over, however, and at least two possible discrepancies between BR practice and the requirements of the 1962 Act looked like remaining unresolved until the TUCC hearings in 1986. The first concerned West Coast main line trains which had been timetabled to use the Settle-Carlisle when engineering work was taking place. BR had failed, as the Act the required, to advertise the alternative service for passengers whose trains would hitherto have been diverted for this reason over the Settle-Carlisle. Indeed BR had already ceased to use the Settle-Carlisle for diverted services except in "emergencies" earlier in 1984, prompting the Yorkshire TUCC to note that it was "most irregular" to withdraw a service in this way in the course of closure proceedings. The "alternative service" which BR should, arguably, have advertised was a bus link between Preston and Lancaster, for example, or -- in the case of Anglo-Scottish traffic -- rail diversion via the East Coast route on the other side of the country.

The second outstanding question concerned the more general point that in three attempts BR had failed to publish one comprehensive closure notice which complied in all respects with the requirements of the 1962 Act. Whether these legal points will have a bearing on the eventual outcome of proceedings remains, as I write, to be seen.

One thing is certain, the try-try-again charade helped push the Settle-Carlisle issue further into the public eye, and among national lobbies to join the protest were Friends of the Earth, who made Appleby station a call on their cycle ride from Land's End to John O'Groats, and the Ramblers Association who held a rally at Settle led by their president, singer-comedian Mike Harding who lives in the Dales.

There remains just one more legal complication to mention -- the Department of Trade's decision to merge the North-East and the Yorkshire TUCC areas, planned originally for Autumn 1984. News of this merger had initially been greeted with dismay by campaigners because it also involved the transfer of responsibility for the Craven district of North Yorkshire (including Skipton and Settle) to the North-West Area TUCC. It was generally believed that the Yorkshire TUCC was prepared to adopt a much more flexible attitude in its consideration of closure proposals than its Manchester-based counterpart and many saw the makings of a thinly disguised attempt to thwart a broad-based consideration of the issues involved in the Settle-Carlisle. In the event, the Yorkshire/North-East merger was deferred to April 1985 and the Skipton transfer was put off until after the Settle-Carlisle hearings.

Feeding Swaledale sheep above Artengill viaduct -- John and Eliza
Forder.

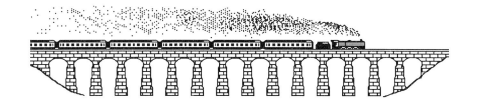

5. A tale of two committees

THIS is the story of how two arms of the Central Transport Consultative Committee interpret their role under the parliamentary Act which governs the procedure for closing railways. Transport Users' Consultative Committees were set up under the 1947 Transport Act and their terms of reference were modified in the Railways Act of 1962. Despite their all-encompassing name, these committees act virtually exclusively as a "watchdog" on British Rail and enjoy the power to make representations to, and demand explanation from BR on a range of issues apart from line closures.

Members of the various independent regional committees which belong to the central body are appointed by the Government from nominations made by a variety of organisations including local authorities, trades unions, commerce and industry, women's organisations, groups representing the elderly and disabled, and tourist authorities.

The length of the Settle-Carlisle line and the route it follows has meant that no fewer than three different regional transport users' committees have become involved in consideration of BR plans to close it. As explained in the previous chapter, the protracted closure proceedings in progress as this book was written have seen changes in the regional organisation of the TUCCs. The various committees were due nonetheless to complete the Settle-Carlisle proceedings on which they had already embarked (in practice all the objections received by the former North-East committee were to be considered by the North-West one). Thus the fact that Craven -- which, with Cumbria, accounts for all but three miles of the Settle-Carlisle --

now falls within the sphere of the North-West committee is of relevance only should the line find itself reprieved in 1986 but be proposed for closure by BR again at a later date.

Nonetheless, this switch of power from York to Manchester has aroused some passion among objectors to the Settle-Carlisle closure. Why should this be and is such apprehension justified? Let's begin with two anecdotes which touch on two areas of the TUCCs' brief. One concerns the meaning of the word "hardship", the hardship likely to be caused to rail users by the withdrawal of services being the subject on which the TUCCs are required to report to the Government. The other area is the extent to which the TUCC can hear and report on evidence not directly related to questions of hardship. First, then, a tale about the TUCC for North-East England, formerly the Yorkshire Area TUCC....

The August 1985 issue of Modern Railways carried a report on the TUCC's deliberations over BR's application to close a stretch of line between Leeds and Sheffield, one of three roughly parallel routes between Yorkshire's first and second cities. It ran thus:

"A remarkable interpretation of the role of the Transport Users' Consultative Committees in hearing objections was provided by the report of the TUCC for North-East England on the proposed withdrawal of passenger services from the line between Goose Hill Junction, Normanton and the former Wath Road Junction near Rotherham, plus the short spur off the line to Oakenshaw Junction, near Wakefield. The TUCC found that a degree of hardship would be caused to users of trains diverted occasionally over the line, although BR did not provide details of the number of trains so affected. A degree of hardship was also attributed to travellers between Leeds and Sheffield 'who would not have the benefits of improved services using all or part of the routes proposed for closure'. These improved services were entirely theoretical and assumed investment in the infrastructure of the line as proposed by objectors, and an increase in the number of trains between Leeds and Sheffield and the possibility of an InterCity station at Cudworth."

On the face of it, the TUCC's conclusions appear to stand the commonly accepted definition of "hardship" on its head, but this probably says more about the TUCC than it does about the precise etymology of the word. When I put it to TUCC Chairman James Towler that his committee's definition of hardship was perhaps rather broader than that of the Oxford English Dictionary, he replied with what seemed a twinkle in his eye: "I stick very closely to the Chamber's Dictionary definition which I think mentions the word 'privation'." A quick check under "privation" shows that following Chamber's can broaden the interpretation of the 62 Act to encompass such loose concepts as "loss or lack of something".

"The role of a TUCC was spelled out very clearly to me by the Treasury Solicitor at the Department of Transport when he said 'TUCCs are transport **users'** consultative committees and their role is to represent the views of rail users'," said Mr Towler. "The members are fully aware of the role of the committee and I can't recall any issue we have had which has not been agreed unanimously."

So how had the committee reached its conclusion on the Goose Hill-Wath Road closure proposal and how did Mr Towler feel about what seemed the rather sarcastic tone of the Modern Railways report? "Now there's a situation where the committee was very conscious of the fact that the service had been run down and run down until it hardly represented a service at all and the committee felt they had to take cognisance of that," he said. He referred me to Dr Roger Bullivant's reply to the Modern Railways item which appeared as a letter in the October 1985 issue and read as follows: "How is the following plan for the closure of a line as exemplified by this route between Sheffield and Leeds, to be prevented?

"1) Run a bad service, for which there will obviously be little demand, for a number of years. Sheffield-Leeds has been described as 'the worst inter-city link in Europe', and a British Rail spokesman is reported to have said that there is 'little demand' for trains between Sheffield and Leeds.

"2) Divert everything except a single summer Saturday holiday train over an inferior route (in this case via Moorthorpe). So bad was the service on the main line that the diversion will not be too noticeable.

"3) Publish a closure proposal claiming (quite truthfully) that 'only one summer Saturday train will be affected'.

"4) Close the line.

"In these circumstances the TUCC was surely right to relate the closure proposal not to the atrocious service actually run over the line, which no doubt few people will miss, but to the reasonable service which should -- and anywhere else in the country would -- have been run between two large cities."

Over to Mr Towler again: "In many ways it comes back to how you interpret the Transport Act and I think there's been a tendency in the past for people to insert words that aren't actually there. People said 'you can only consider hardship' and it became sort of folk lore. The Act says TUCCs consider **the objection**....the word 'only' does not appear. The grounds for objection are wide open -- we are obliged to report to the Minister on hardship but as the act does not **only** say hardship the Yorkshire committee takes the view that this does not preclude us from drawing the Minister's attention to other issues where there is considerable public interest."

The foregoing would appear to epitomise how Mr Towler's committee sees itself: here is the railway users' Clark Kent, emerging becaped from the station toilets to swoop to the aid of the hapless traveller marooned at some long-forgotten halt somewhere between Fitzwilliam and Featherstone.

But what about the North-West TUCC?

As already suggested, subscribers to the conspiracy theory of government saw in the June 1984 plans to reorganise the TUCC boundaries a plot to lessen the chances of a Settle-Carlisle victory -- if not in the current closure fight then certainly in any future one. Rightly or wrongly, the North-West Area TUCC -- in the shadow perhaps of its Yorkshire neighbour, whose oft quoted chairman's remarks were frequently far from sympathetic to British Rail -- had failed (or not chosen) to gain a similar reputation as the champion of the passenger's cause. The Settle-Carlisle Joint Action Committee chairman John Whitelegg put it like this: "It [the North-West TUCC] does not aggressively defend the interests of rail transport -- it sees its role as pouring oil on troubled waters." This, he felt, was in contrast to the stance adopted east of the Pennines and he went on: "The North-West TUCC does not inspire confidence in my organisation."

I put Dr Whitelegg's charge to the North-West TUCC and received this reply: "We are just here as arbitrators -- we are not here to stick up for the railway or the public. The Transport Act says we look at it under the hardship it [closure] would cause. It has been broadcast for some while that there is a difference of opinion [between the North-West and the Yorkshire committees] -- we are sticking to the statute."

As a result of those interviews I wrote a piece for the Yorkshire Post which quoted Dr Whitelegg as saying the North-West committee "adopted a less 'pro-rail' attitude" than its Yorkshire counterpart. Other newspapers carried similar quotes around that time and soon afterwards Dr Whitelegg found himself invited to Manchester to meet members of the North-West TUCC, giving what he anticipated would be a useful opportunity for an exchange of views. What actually greeted him was a rather less egalitarian gathering than he had anticipated.

"A collection of press cuttings was thrust across the table at me and I was asked to explain myself," he recalled. As the members made it clear they were less than pleased with the remarks attributed to Dr Whitelegg, the meeting -- chaired by magistrate Olive Clarke -- became increasingly inquisitorial to the point where Dr Whitelegg was forced to issue a reminder that having attended of his own free will he was equally free to walk out when he chose and would not hesitate to do so. "I twice got up to leave," he said. The meeting eventually moved to a more constructive close, with the committee inviting Dr Whitelegg to join them for lunch. But if oil had been poured on troubled waters, a mischievous gremlin was busy adding detergent: in taking him to a Berni steak house, the poor committee had failed to allow for the possibility that their guest might be a vegetarian. The resultant embarrassment can be left to the imagination!

These two stories may give an inkling as to the workings of the two bodies which were due play a key role in deciding the fate of the Settle and Carlisle. To try and assess to what extent any fears on the part of objectors might be grounded, I arranged to meet the chairs of the two committees face-to-face in the run-up to the 1986 Settle-Carlisle hearings.

Speculation that the Government might see in the inauguration of the new TUCC for North-East England the opportunity to ditch the troublesome Mr Towler and perhaps enjoy a lower-key, Towler-free Settle-Carlisle hearing had proved ill-founded when the outgoing chairman of the old Yorkshire Area TUCC was appointed by the Secretary of State in April 1985 to head the new body for two years. "So unless the proverbial bus comes along it looks like I'm going to be about," said Mr Towler as we pulled out of Settle bang on time on the 10.00 for Carlisle. At a time when he was heavily committed conducting the hearing into the proposed closure of the Huddersfield to Denby Dale link, Mr Towler suggested we could squeeze in a meeting by riding up to Appleby and returning on the morning train to Leeds.

It was a glorious day, the late October sunshine casting a clear light across the fells and revealing their massive beauty in a way which can rarely be enjoyed in the mid-summer haze. The platform had been busy, with a good number of families obviously taking advantage of the half-term break to see at first hand what all this Settle-Carlisle fuss was about. "This train left Settle with 402 people last Saturday," said Mr Towler as he disappeared to do a head-count, which turned out at 190 -- not bad for a Thursday.

The hazards of journeying on an under-used railway soon became apparent as we pulled out of the town and entered the cutting which marks the start of the so-called Long Drag -- 15 miles of almost continuous climb at a gradient of one-in-100. The locomotive's wheels were slipping on the rails, still wet with dew despite the passage of the early diesel multiple unit. We proceeded at snail's pace until the combination of emerging into sunlight and the brief levelling of the track in the Ribble gorge at Helwith Bridge enabled us finally to gain some momentum. "I came to be in this job many years ago in the early 70s when I was a member of the Confederation of British Industry's regional committee," said Mr Towler. He had put his name forward in response to an invitation to the CBI to nominate someone to serve on the TUCC -- the youthful vigour with which this amiable father-of-one appears to pursue his job seems far from the stereotype of the CBI man of around 50. "Like most other kids just after the war I collected train numbers, and shortly after I went into long trousers my train numbers went out of the window." His more recent railway experiences came as chairman of the family's small engineering company and as a non-executive director of Pennine Radio at Bradford, in which capacities he has travelled frequently from New Pudsey, near Leeds, to London and elsewhere.

James Towler

"I do appreciate the benefits of rail travel more than I did before, particularly as a businessman, because it's possible to work on the train," he said. "I deplore the way BR has done away with the First Class day return, because if the conditions are not suitable for working, I might as well go by car. I prefer to go by train, but I go to Nottingham by coach because, due to the re-routeing of the Nottingham-Glasgow trains, the coach is better."

Mr Towler believes he became TUCC chairman almost by default when there was a vacancy soon after the election of the first Thatcher Government in 1979. He had by then been elected deputy chairman by the committee. "There was some doubt as to the future of the TUCCs at that time and I think there was a feeling that as the job might not last too long you might as well let the deputy do it rather than bring in someone from the great outside." But notwithstanding misgivings about the TUCCs at both ends of the political spectrum, any doubts about their future failed to be translated into their demise and Mr Towler remained chairman.

The TUCCs are responsible to the Department of Trade and

their members are ministerial appointments made in consultation with the chairmen and women. Only the chairman's post is paid, the other members receiving out-of-pocket expenses. "The chairmanship is a part-time job which is taking a great deal of my time," said Mr Towler. "I work from home, and burning the midnight oil, one endeavours to keep on top of it." While confessing the nominal one-day-a-week job had become somewhat more time-consuming, Mr Towler suggested his opposite number on the East of England Area TUCC devoted even more time to the job than he did.

What has taken so much of Mr Towler's time has been the relatively large number of closures his committee has had to consider. Mr Towler began to count them off on his fingers: "There was the Humber ferry and its associated rail links; Huddersfield to Sheffield 'mark one'; Goose Hill to Wath Road; the so-called Five Curves [a collection of links between various routes in West Yorkshire]; and Goole to Gilberdyke. We are currently on Huddersfield to Denby Dale [on the Sheffield route] 'mark two'; then we have Leeds to Castleford and Normanton via the direct route. There is no doubt that there have been more railway closure proposals since 1979/80 in this part of the world than in all the rest of the country put together."

Mr Towler continued: "The role of the TUCC is tending to develop -- the situation today is not what it was in the Beeching era. In the Beeching era, with one or two exceptions like the old Great Central and the Waverley route, the closures related to branch lines which, sadly, weren't used very much. So when the closure came up there were relatively few objections. The economy was expanding, as was car ownership, and -- in political terms -- somebody said we had never had it so good.

"Now the branch lines have gone and the scenario is different. I suppose car ownership will tend to increase, although I don't suppose it's increasing at the same rate.... so I think that now, when there is a proposal to discontinue a railway service, people are genuinely more concerned at the proposal and are prepared to lodge objections. Because, by and large the lines proposed for closure recently are well patronised or else the service has been run down to such an extent by re-routeing etcetera that objectors can claim that BR are indulging in closure by stealth." A classic case, said Mr Towler, was that Goose Hill to Wath Road section of the old fast route to Sheffield.

So is this "willingness to take on British Rail" and "combative attitude on behalf of the traveller" as described in Modern Railways, April 1985, a product of the Yorkshire TUCC's special circumstances? "The TUCCs enjoy a degree of autonomy and independence working within the Act, which I would not wish to see undermined," said Mr Towler. "So I would no more think of telling another TUCC chairman how to operate his business than I would expect him to tell me how to conduct mine. On the other hand, when it comes to closure proposals I think that it's a fact that in recent years the former Yorkshire committee and myself have had more experience of closure proposals than the other TUCCs. "Our feeling is that we should interpret the Act fairly, but any ambiguities should be interpreted in favour of the user."

After an all-too-brief stop at the magnificently kept station at Appleby, we joined 94 others on the southbound train and got down to the nitty-gritty of the committee's day-to-day work. This concerns nothing so dramatic as railway closures and Mr Towler has found it convenient to divide the new North-East TUCC into three area sub-committees to handle routine matters such as complaints about services and timetables. The normal cycle sees at least three meetings of each sub-committee annually and a similar number for the main committee -- the Settle-Carlisle closure proposal has, needless to say, imposed a massive extra workload on the committee. "It's the secretary's job to read each and every objection and he draws up the summary of objections under lots of different headings," said Mr Towler who can claim, in line with his preferred policy, to have actually read most of the 14,000-odd individual objections lodged. In addition, he helped process some of the objections because of the sheer volume of work required. "When you are dealing with anything regarding British Rail you have to get down to detail, whether it's timetables or fare structure, so it does mean quite a lot of graft," said Mr Towler.

This instinctive distrust of BR is something that surfaces frequently when talking with Mr Towler -- it bobbed up again when we got on to the implications of the "any user affected" discovery which, as explained in the previous chapter, had opened the door to a much broader field of objectors, including DalesRail passengers, and those using services for which the Settle-Carlisle might provide a diversionary route. "It's very difficult sometimes dealing with BR when trying to get over points which to most people appear relatively simple and straightforward," he said. "We went ahead with the Goose Hill-Wath Road hearing when the legal advice given to me independently was that the closure notice didn't comply with the Act." After much time and money had been expended BR had reached a similar conclusion and the procedure had been restarted.

So supposing somebody chose to challenge the validity of the Settle-Carlisle composite closure notice? "There are those who argue that none of the three closure notices fully complies with the terms of Section 56," said Mr Towler. "I take the view that anything can happen but I would hope when we go ahead with our hearing that people don't take steps to delay or interrupt the hearings, because basically we want to hear what people have got to say and a lot of planning goes into a public hearing. Some people will be taking a week of their holiday to attend so it would be unfair on objectors who wish to make representations to the committee if they found the hearing had to be deferred because someone had decided to issue an injunction to prevent it

"On the other hand, it's a free country and if any individual or any body feels they have a legitimate grievance which they can rectify by a resort to the law, they are fully entitled to do so."

Pictured, right, by Ian Jopson, Lord Nelson crosses Dent Head viaduct from the North in March 1984. The panorama typifies the scenery crossed in the line's central section.

He pointed out that we were talking about a public hearing, not an inquiry: "The purpose of the public hearing is so that the committee can hear oral evidence and the views and opinions of the objectors. Given that the committee is obliged to report to the minister on hardship, it's eminently sensible that those objectors who feel they will suffer hardship should concentrate on that." In practice, he said, this meant a mix of evidence on hardship and other considerations; and a mix between individual objectors and those representing bodies such as local authorities. "We heard 50 objectors in a two-and-a-half-hour session at the Huddersfield-Denby Dale hearing," said Mr Towler. And if that sounds a lot, he added: "I try and ensure that everybody gets an opportunity to say what they want to say."

We emerge suddenly from the black of Blea Moor tunnel into the brown expanse of Blea Moor, with Whernside on our right beautifully lit by the mid-day sun -- a different world from the pastel greens of Dentdale we left little over a minute and a mile-and-a-quarter behind us. "Each time I travel on this line I see something I haven't seen before," says Mr Towler. "The Eden valley is so different from the moorland we see up here." As we slow down for the speed restriction over Ribblehead, there remains just time to touch on the question of cross-examination which, because of certain legal judgements, looked at the time of writing as though it could prove a key issue at the hearings.

"The position we adopt is that people can ask questions of BR through the chair and I will give BR an opportunity to reply," said Mr Towler. "If they choose not to reply to a question, I can't force them to reply." He felt there was a strong case for requiring British Rail to supply more financial information: "In their remit, the TUCCs can put forward suggestions for alleviating hardship -- it would be helpful to know more details of the sums of money involved so we don't put forward suggestions for alleviating hardship which could possibly be more expensive than keeping the line open." In the 60s, in response to an investigation ordered by the then Minister of Transport Ernest Marples, BR had been publishing the level of support provided for each line. Changed accounting procedures had seen the end of the practice, much to Mr Towler's ire: "If you have got a good case in any walk of life you should be able to back it with figures. Here we are dealing with public bodies -- it's only right that figures should be made known to the public, not even just the TUCCs." All of which led Mr Towler to conclude, as we pulled into Settle: "I think they must consider we are a bit of a pain in the arse -- but then we would not be doing our job properly if we weren't. At many levels I like to think there is a great deal of mutual respect."

If meeting James Towler demanded conjuring a free day out of his full diary, securing an interview with his North-West counterpart, Olive Clarke, would provide an even greater challenge. Mrs Clarke, MBE, JP, has what lesser mortals might consider a quite unenviable list of commitments -- besides chairing the TUCC, she has served on Kendal magistrates' bench for 25 years and is chairman of the juvenile court and of the South Cumbria Magistrates Association; she is chairman of the Westmorland and Furness Country Landowners Association and a member of the association's national legal and parliamentary committee; she is chairman of the governors of her village school and a governor of Cumbria College of Agriculture and Forestry; she is life vice-president of the Young Farmers Club, president of Northern Counties Young Farmers, president-elect of the Westmorland Show and a commissioner for the Inland Revenue. In anticipation of her Settle-Carlisle workload, she retired in Autumn 1985 from the review committee for parole at Durham jail where she was also Deputy Chairman of the Board of Visitors. The use of the word chair"man" is by her choice rather than the author's.

As if that impressive list were not enough, she was busily preparing to fulfil a lifetime's ambition by spending Christmas with her husband crossing Australia by train. Nonetheless, having overcome her initial reticence about speaking to the Press, a few days later saw me pulling up outside the neat white farmhouse, complete with magnificent monkey puzzle tree, Albert the peacock, and his mate Victoria. A few hundred yards away the M6 ripped through the rolling hills at the edge of Lakeland, its thundering traffic oblivious to this serene other world.

A lively, neatly-dressed woman of 60, Mrs Clarke told me over coffee and home-made shortbread how she had been appointed to the TUCC in 1967 after being nominated by the National Women's Institute, an organisation of which she was county chairman. "I was brought up when times were very bad. I was a farmer's only child but I won a scholarship to a good girls' school," she said, having once got the better of the telephone's interruptions. Married to a farmer in 1947, she is the mother of two daughters and proud grandmother of four. A self-confessed workaholic, she said: "I have succeeded in a man's world -- but I am an old fashioned wife." Her view of women's liberation was that a husband's needs should remain paramount -- if she was not there to cook for him she would ensure someone else was. And if women could come to terms with their lot in this way, she said, they would have much happier marriages.

Mrs Clarke has spent her whole life in just two houses: "A lot of people can go and live somewhere and leave their past behind," she said. "If you live where you have always been it's more difficult." But despite such deep roots, her numerous posts had, she said, necessitated a good deal of travelling and enabled her to learn a lot about people -- ideal preparation for assuming the TUCC chair, as she did in 1979.

"When you think of the job it is, after all, one concerned with people and getting things right or better for people," she said. "If they do have a complaint and they don't get satisfaction from British Rail then they have somewhere else to go where they will get a fair hearing. Clearly it's essential with a big nationalised industry like British Rail that they can't just say 'well that bit doesn't pay' or 'we want to close this bit'. There must be a body like the TUCC to hear what people say -- railways are here for the benefit of people and I see my role very much bound up with the well-being of people."

Strong words! And hardly the sort of tone you'd expect from someone alleged not to be the vigorous champion of the railway passenger. Perhaps the difference between hers and Mr Towler's committee is at a more philosophical level: "I am a great believer that you will catch more flies with molasses than you ever will with vinegar," she said. "And that's been my attitude with British Rail -- there's no point in shouting the odds and being awkward." Certainly, the North-West TUCCs annual reports do not shy away from giving praise to BR where praise is felt to be due, and can list the restoration of timetable cuts on various local services among concessions the committee's representations have won. "I feel it is essential to have a good working relationship with BR -- that does not mean that we are oblivious to their faults. I don't see the job as being against each other but working together for the good of the passenger."

Her own area of concern is the London sleeper service which she believes is essential for anywhere above a certain distance from the capital -- but she has seen usage on the Preston-Euston sleeper decline to the point where she sees its long-term future in question.

Mrs Clarke describes herself as a "relic of the Beeching era" and remembers sitting on closure hearings in the 60s with monotonous regularity -- some of the lines mooted for the axe are long gone, others, like the Windermere branch, are still there today. She remembers well the hearings which led to the loss of the local service on the Settle-Carlisle. "There had to be closure of a lot of lines in this country," she said. "Whether mistakes were made and whether it was a matching process all over the country is another question -- one thing I rejoice in is the number of stations that have been o p e n e d in the North-West.....More coffee?"

Despite the complexity of a vast area stretching from the Scottish border to the High Peak area of Derbyshire, the North-West TUCC has not had the rash of recent closure proposals seen east of the Pennines. Mrs Clarke remains nonetheless clear of the committee's role in such circumstances: "We do **not** recommend on closure -- the committee does not take the decision -- that is the responsibility of the minister. The TUCCs are made up of lay people representative of the area -- they are there simply to listen and report to the Minister on the hardship that would be caused should the closure take place." The word "hardship", she said, was interpreted "in its broadest sense".

But the TUCC's report was just one channel of information from which the minister would draw in making his decision on the future of a line. Thus, in the case of the Settle-Carlisle, she said: "We have been asking people who wish to object on a variety of grounds to write to the Minister -- there is nothing ministers love more than getting a deluge of letters on the table! All the people who are on about the beautiful scenery should write to the minister because it's a question of national heritage."

She continued: "I am not trying to stifle progress, but this is not a public inquiry -- it's a public hearing and there's a tremendous difference." The committee could not change the way it considered closure proposals unless the Act itself was changed, she stressed.

As with the TUCC for North-East England, the North-West committee, which normally meets five times a year, has been all but overwhelmed by the volume of work created by the Settle-Carlisle hearing: "We have had two-and-a-half tons of paper come into the office to be sent out with the next lot of stuff," said Mrs Clarke. "And we're up on the third floor!" She concluded: "This is something about which we all care deeply -- about the antiquity, the heritage, and the fact that it's there, and we're clearly conscious of the responsibilities."

So, looking ahead from the time of writing, are there likely to be significant differences in the way the two TUCCs conduct their hearings into the Settle-Carlisle closure in March and April 1986? It seems fair to say that the TUCC for North-East England is likely to admit a broad range of evidence which it will forward as appendices to its report. The North-West view is clearly that such evidence should be sent direct to the Secretary of State. Correspondence from the Secretary of State to objectors interested in broadening the issues considered by the TUCCs seems to uphold the North-West interpretation. But it would be wrong to presume that **either** committee will give objectors carte blanche to present huge volumes of oral evidence, particularly where it is backed up by written reports.

The Settle-Carlisle Joint Action Committee has stated it requires ten days to present its evidence: such a concession appears at the time of writing most unlikely, particularly given that the dates fixed provisionally for the hearings allow only 13 days in total. While Mr Towler and Mrs Clarke appear willing to permit some extension to that, both are conscious that their committees are made up of lay members who have work and other commitments. The North-West committee in particular stresses the need to hear pleadings of hardship first and would prefer complex reports on other issues to be sent direct to the Minister. As the Joint Action Committee sees the hearings as an opportunity to present its evidence in the full glare of publicity, this solution is most unlikely to be seen as satisfactory.

The Joint Action Committee has repeatedly argued for a full public inquiry to ensure that objectors get the opportunity to cross-examine British Rail witnesses -- and for that matter to expose their own case to the test of cross-examination by BR. In that they have some sympathy from Mrs Clarke. "One could argue whether this [a TUCC hearing] is the right means in modern times to consider a very intricate closure," she said. "I have no opinions on whether a public inquiry would be best but I can see their view." She continued: "The law has not been altered and until the law is altered this is the system, and I feel that the Act is adequate as it stands."

It is worth noting that there is nothing to stop the Secretary of State ordering a public inquiry or a judicial review after he has considered the submissions from the TUCCs, although that is perhaps unlikely given the costs involved. Indeed it is not unreasonable to speculate that Mr Towler's renewed chairmanship might have been calculated by the Minister as a suitable sop to objectors lest they should seek to make capital of any more rigid interpretation of the Act by the North-West committee. Certainly it is curious that Mr Towler should have been appointed for just two years at the same time as Mrs Clarke was given a new three-year term and it is tempting to equate those two years with the likely duration of the closure proceedings.

It is also worth considering what might happen if the TUCC for North-East England were to exercise its option to submit its own report should any major differences between the two committees emerge, on the interpretation of hardship, say. A "pro-Settle-Carlisle" report from the North-West TUCC might well carry more weight in Whitehall than one from Mr Towler's committee, of which the pro-rail stance is well known.

The TUCCs are now nearly 40 years old and there is a wide body of opinion which maintains it is unjust that a mechanism designed to deal with the closure of the odd few miles of branch railway should be applied to a 72-miles main line, albeit an under-used one. Additionally, criticisms of the TUCCs' narrow remit are typified by Mayer Hillman and Anne Whalley in their study, The Social Consequences of Rail Closure: "The dividing line between hardship and inconvenience does appear to be very thin and capable of being moved back and forth according to who is experiencing the effect, its cause, its duration, and whether or not it can be alleviated." While there has been a powerful lobby seeking a Parliamentary solution to the problem, there were also important legal attempts in 1985 to clarify the workings of the existing system.

In one, objectors to the withdrawal of services from Tunbridge Wells to Eridge sought a judicial review of the TUCC evidence -- only for BR to remove the track before this was complete! A second case stemmed from the London Regional Passengers' Committee's consideration of British Rail plans to close Marylebone station. The LRPC is the capital's TUCC and Brent and three other Tory-controlled London boroughs, the Greater London Council and Buckinghamshire County Council went to the High Court to seek a judicial review after the LRPC refused to permit counsel representing the local authorities to cross-examine BR and make final submissions on their behalf.

Although Mr Justice Kennedy dismissed the application for a judicial review in a decision which was subsequently upheld at appeal, he did make a number of observations which could clarify procedure at the Settle-Carlisle and other hearings. The more important points were:

☐ All sides should know the case they have to answer -- this would impose some burden on BR, for example, to furnish accurate and "honest" financial data.

☐ There is a good case for both sides to have the right to make a final submission at the end of proceedings -- while Mr

Towler's committee has customarily allowed an objector the last word at hearings, some other TUCCs have allowed BR to have the final say.

□ Where TUCCs do allow cross-examination, the questions should be asked by someone is technically competent.

□ TUCC chairmen and women should not "unduly fetter" themselves by establishing inflexible rules of procedure which might, for example, preclude the possibility of cross-examination should the need arise.

The Brent action should be seen as part of a broader political campaign which has seen a remarkable cross-party unity typified by the joint approach of the Labour-led Association of Metropolitan Authorities and the Association of County Councils (Tory-led when the approach began, but "hung" at the time of writing) in lobbying for a public inquiry procedure to replace the TUCCs in dealing with rail closure proposals.

Prominent among the metropolitan authorities in this campaign has been West Yorkshire County Council which was quick to find common cause with Cumbria in questioning the adequacy of the 1962 Railways Act for dealing with such a major closure proposal as the Settle-Carlisle. A report from the Cumbria County Planning Officer in December 1983 stated: "The present procedures were established during a period when the wider implications of such decisions were less appreciated and when a very large exercise of pruning the rail system was to ensue from the Beeching Report of 1963.

"Now, when the ramifications of such decisions are understood to be very far reaching, when these issues may establish important precedents for remaining parts of the secondary rail network in remote and rural areas, it is time that the procedure should be properly revised to encompass all relevant matters. This has clearly been seen to be the case at inquiries in major developments such as a third London airport and Sizewell B nuclear power station. There is no reason why it should not apply also to the proposed closure of important public facilities and services, which may also influence future investment decisions."

West Yorkshire County Council subsequently acquired the

support of the AMA in calling for the scope of the TUCC hearings to be widened to consider issues apart from hardship, namely:

☐ Freight, as well as passenger traffic

☐ The financial performance of the line, including "contributory" revenue generated at stations on other lines

☐ The scope for improvement in the line's financial performance

☐ The importance of the line in the local economy

☐ National and local government transport and railway policies.

It was also suggested that if the changes were adopted it might be better for inquiries to be conducted by an independent inspector rather than the TUCCs.

The AMA duly arranged for an amendments to be tabled in the committee stages of Transport Bill in both Houses of Parliament. These called for the replacement of TUCC hearings with a full inquiry as required in the case of road closures under the Highways Act and the Town and Country Planning Act; a mandatory public inquiry in cases where objections were lodged by local authorites; the specification of matters the Secretary of State should consider before reaching his decision; the extension of procedures to include freight lines.

The amendments were not accepted by the Government and the AMA and the ACC subsequently made a detailed joint submission to the Under-Secretary of State for Transport, David Mitchell, pointing out the iniquity of the TUCC system when compared with "the appropriately thorough and wide-ranging examination" customary under town planning legislation.

Mr Mitchell met a joint delegation from the AMA and the ACC at the Department of Transport's Marsham Street offices in October 1985 when the apparent shortcomings of the TUCC procedure were put to him. West Yorkshire County Council's public transport office chief John Carr stressed the wide discrepancy in the interpretation of the word "hardship" by the various committees and in the extent to which they would allow evidence not strictly related to hardship. He also raised the contention that BR was often accused -- with apparent justification -- of manipulating the procedure to indulge in "closure by stealth" as exemplified by the Leeds-Sheffield route earlier in this chapter.

While the Minister did not accept the case for a major change to a procedure which had "stood the test of time", he did promise to consider with his officials a "spring clean". He also clarified other points

-- that it was Government policy that there should be no major programme of route closures

-- that TUCCs had direct access to the Minister on matters of major concern through the Central Transport Consultative Committee

-- that he would consider giving TUCC chairmen guidance to ensure his attention was drawn to matters other than hardship which were raised at hearings

-- that local authorities had direct access to the Minister on wider considerations than hardship.

He also felt a case had been made out for the TUCCs to ensure that their role was more fully understood by the public. Mr Carr commented afterwards: "Probably rather more progress was made than had originally been expected." Meanwhile, West Yorkshire County Council and its Cumbrian and Lancastrian partners were continuing, at the time of writing, to lobby for a Parliamentary debate on the Settle-Carlisle closure plan.

Above: Under-Secretary of State for Transport David Mitchell
takes a look for himself at the condition of Ribblehead viaduct.
Yorkshire Post picture.
Below: Ribblehead -- a study in limestone, by John and Eliza
Forder.

6. Wanton neglect

THE introduction to this book told how leaders of Cumbria and West Yorkshire county councils announced their decision to commission a firm of top transport consultants to conduct an independent appraisal of the Settle-Carlisle line, its structures and its potential for the future. Subsequent chapters will have given some idea why the councils, and the other authorities who joined them, felt it was imperative that British Rail should not enjoy a monopoly in the presentation of information which would have a bearing on the future of the route.

On July 26, 1984, Professor Donald MacKay rose to tell a press conference at County Hall, Kendal, the findings of his Edinburgh-based firm's six-month survey. PEIDA had been chosen for the job because -- as the head of West Yorkshire's Public Transport Office, John Carr, put it -- "their presentation was by the far the best we received". But PEIDA also had a sound "track record" to complement its professional packaging. The company had previously been called in by the Highlands and Islands Development Board to conduct an assessment of the remote Inverness to Kyle of Lochalsh line which was threatened with closure in the 1970s.

"At that time the Kyle line was in the same situation that this line is in now," Prof. MacKay had told me on board the Cumbrian Mountain Express Press special, seven months previously. "Our study suggested that the economics were a good deal more favourable and the usage much higher than BR's figures." PEIDA found the figures had omitted key elements such as journeys by people on "Rover-style" and other special tickets. The line was subsequently reprieved and investment made in it, including the provision of radio signalling.

But anyone who thought PEIDA would simply pour a bucket of liberal economic whitewash over the Settle-Carlisle to come up with the answers the counties wanted to hear would have realised with only a little research that this was unlikely to prove to be the case. Donald MacKay -- professorial fellow at Heriot-Watt University -- is well known to readers of the quality daily, The Scotsman, for his regular column on economics. You don't need to know your Keynes from your Friedman to recognise the writings of a committed monetarist. In the broadest sense, and one should be wary of the glib use of labels, Prof. MacKay appears to belong to that rising intellectual school of the 80s, the New Right. While the externally expressed political views of the PEIDA senior partner had no bearing whatsoever on the appointment of the firm, the councils could at least feel secure their survey team would be talking the same economic language as the Government and British Rail. Prof. MacKay defined his personal views on the subject thus: "I believe in an efficient, cost-effective method of public transport." And John Gunnell, the leader of West Yorkshire County Council, summarised exactly what his own authority and Cumbria were after: "We want a decision to be taken on the basis of fact rather than sentiment."

County Coun. Gunnell got the facts he wanted -- but Prof. MacKay's words at the Kendal press conference also included some pretty damning comment. The professor told the conference PEIDA had drawn a similar conclusion to BR insofar as retention of the Settle-Carlisle would involve continued operating losses and substantial capital expenditure. But the fact that the required expenditure was as high as it was, was due in considerable part to BR's own policy. Prof. MacKay said he was choosing his words carefully in accusing BR of being guilty of "wanton neglect" of the Settle-Carlisle line.

"British Rail has simply not carried out the level of work necessary to keep the capital structure in good order and that imposes substantial future costs that would have been avoided if BR had acted sensibly," said Prof. MacKay. Indeed, maintenance on the line since 1980 had been minimal and BR had allowed repairs to mount so that about £17.5m. would have to be spent simply to retain a single-track railway, said the professor. "The major contributory factor to the deficit has been the financial policy followed by British Rail itself -- in effect, BR determined to close this line some years ago and has proceeded on the basis that it would close. And so BR's policy has been to carry out on the line only the most minimum work necessary for safety purposes -- it has not carried out good husbandry."

British Rail's Settle-Carlisle Project Manager Ron Cotton rejected the "wanton neglect" allegation, but said: "Like any other business organisation we have not been investing in an area where there is some indecision as to the future." To have acted otherwise would have been "reprehensible" in the circumstances, he said.

Prof. Donald MacKay pictured by Barry Wilkinson/Picture House

While the PEIDA report clearly did not show BR in a particularly good light, it did in many ways support the general BR thesis, namely that the line was unlikely to generate an operating profit. In doing so it took as read the BR case that the Settle-Carlisle was surplus to main line network requirements and rejected any case for upgrading it to take High Speed Trains. It conceded that a "tourist operated" line might make a profit "but this must be subject to some doubt and any profit would be very small relative to the capital and maintenance costs of the central section".

But leaving aside the question of the backlog of maintenance, PEIDA found that the Settle-Carlisle's performance was not substantially different to that of other lines in the Provincial Sector. By eliminating waste as exemplified by the train costs quoted in Chapter Four (PEIDA found productive train time at 18 per cent was only half the normal level) it was reckoned the annual operating deficit could be brought down to about £205,000.

So Prof. MacKay was able to tell the conference: "The

91

problems are not different in principle or practice from the problems affecting other lines in the UK. The line -- properly maintained and marketed -- is no better or worse than other provincial lines." Logically then, he continued: "If Settle-Carlisle goes it certainly follows on our analysis that other provincial lines will follow -- and quite a number of them." This would run against the practice of successive governments which had been to retain such lines because of the wider benefits they brought which were not apparent in the simple financial returns. There could be "no justification", he said, for "picking off lines piecemeal", starting with the Settle-Carlisle -- a prospect which prompted Wayne Jenkins, West Yorkshire's public transport chairman, to ask: "Are BR trying to implement the Serpell report by stealth?"

It has been argued that the PEIDA report took an unnecessarily narrow view of the Settle-Carlisle and may have been rather conservative in its estimates of the likely returns on marketing investment. Options including reopening some stations, the re-introduction of InterCity services or the privatisation of the line were eliminated to give a simple model involving a single-track railway with efficiency increased by investment in radio signalling and revenue improved through effective marketing. That model was then used as the basis for a "cost-benefit appraisal".

The PEIDA approach was to base the analysis on the firmest evidence available: obviously it could not be assumed InterCity trains would return to the line when the appropriate BR sector had made a policy decision to withdraw them; nor could estimates of likely traffic in the event of successful marketing be pitched too high as there was no empirical data to justify such optimism. It would clearly have been possible to conduct further cost-benefit analyses on a range of other options including all sorts of variables from installing magnetic levitation feeder services to turning the whole lot into a motorway. Having discounted the privatisation/enthusiasts' railway option as being unlikely to match the kind of resources available through BR's Public Service Obligation grant, PEIDA compared the costs and benefits of retaining the most basic railway to fulfil the perceived requirements with the costs and benefits associated with closing the line.

Cost-benefit analysis is a complex procedure which involves giving a monetary value to a variety of factors which, in the case of a railway closure plan, might include the cost to society of the additional journey times people would face, or the cost of road improvements to cater for additional traffic. It also requires making predictions about people's behaviour to establish, for example, the likely loss of revenue which BR would incur if it closed the Settle-Carlisle. As BR had already stated that it intended to retain two stubs of line at either end to serve the ballast quarry railhead at Ribblehead and the Ministry of Defence at Warcop on the old Kirkby Stephen branch from Appleby, PEIDA limited the consideration of engineering costs to those that would be incurred on the central section of the line between Ribblehead and Appleby. (At the time of writing there is some question within BR, said to be unrelated to the Settle-Carlisle question, over the continued use of the Ribblehead railhead.)

Over a 20-year period, said PEIDA, the cost of retaining the line would be £9,899,000 at 1984 prices, whereas the benefits lost by closure would amount to £7,153,000. Thus, as PEIDA's summary report pointed out "there appears to be a marginal case for closing the line". But it stressed this was in the context of the **assumptions adopted** [*PEIDA's emphasis*]. Additionally, there was "inevitable uncertainty" about many of the values in the cost-benefit analysis and there were also factors which were not taken into account. These included individual hardship such as would be considered by the TUCC hearings, wider economic impact (PEIDA envisaged a "major effect" on tourism), and the importance of the line "in heritage terms" as "a prime example of Victorian railway engineering".

Prof. MacKay summed this up at the press conference: "The study demonstrates quite clearly that the closure of the central section of the line would impose real and heavy costs and these are quite close to the costs saved by BR through closure -- the Settle-Carlisle case has to be looked at in the much wider context of the future of British Rail provincial services." The apparent discrepancy between the Secretary of State's pronoucements on this subject and his actual deeds in terms of the PSO grant allocated are discussed in more detail in Chapter Ten.

As already revealed, BR's neglect of the Settle-Carlisle had greatly inflated the costs of keeping it open -- the extent of the engineering problems was considered in a survey for PEIDA by the Leeds-based civil engineers, W.A. Fairhurst and Partners. Their report commented: "The structures on the railway line, having been completed in 1875, should by modern standards be nearing the end of their designed life of 120 years. Despite the remoteness of the route, its altitude and exposure to the ravages of winter weather, the structures have stood the test of time remarkably well and remain in fairly good condition throughout."

But, the report continued: "Inspection demonstrates that many of the structures, particularly the viaducts, are now showing the effects of inadequate maintenance and the failure to carry out timely repairs as a result of insufficient investment funds being made avaialable. Deterioration is much more severe where limestone has been used as the predominant construction material than where sandstone or millstone grit has been used." The most serious cause of deterioration found by Fairhurst's was water, particularly where it had gained access to viaducts through failure of the waterproof membranes below deck level. "The problem has been recognised by BR since the late 1940s but finance has not been provided to replace the waterproofing," said the report. Deterioration had accelerated and, with a parallel further slowing of maintenance through insufficient funding, a point had been reached where "failure to keep pace with maintenance could well result in some structures having to be replaced".

Examples of the sort of make-do repair made on the line are epitomised by the author's observation of an attempt to prevent percolation of water through the aqueduct/tunnel which carries Force Gill over the line at Blea Moor. This consisted of a plastic sheet weighted down by rocks which had, not surprisingly, been substantially dislodged in the course of the depressingly wet 1985 summer.

In all, of the estimated £9,928,000 needed to give the line another 20 years' life, some £5,390,000 would go on repairs to viaducts excluding Ribblehead, repairs to which were costed at £2.1m. If Ribblehead were replaced the bill would rise to £12,278,000. The major problem on the track itself was the condition of many of the wooden sleepers -- on one stretch rotting sleepers had allowed the track gauge to widen by 3/16". But singling the track would allow maximum use to be made of the best remaining stretches while avoiding some of the worst parts. Including the installation of radio signalling, this singling scheme would cost £5,474,000.

In many ways it is misleading to single out Ribblehead viaduct for special attention -- the figures above show it is only one, admittedly significant, element in a large repair bill. The sums concerned become even smaller in the context of London Midland Region or total British Rail maintenance, and smaller still when compared with the billions spent on other parts of the transport infrastructure, notably motorway maintenance. But because British Rail has decided that Ribblehead should be the altar upon which the Settle-Carlisle should be sacrificed it is appropriate to examine how the viaduct came to be in such a sorry state and to what extent the estimates of making good the damage are reasonable. It is worth reminding the reader that it is not unreasonable to expect to have to carry out repairs on structures which are more than 100 years old -- in most organisations there would be adequate budgetry provision to cover such depreciation of assets. It should also be remembered that Ribblehead is in many ways unique -- it combines limestone construction with exposure to one of the harshest climates in England at a point where winds are funnelled at great speed through the Pennines and the effect of freeze-thaw action on the masonry is considerable. The following account of the demise of Ribblehead viaduct is compiled from internal British Rail sources (some of whom can not be named) and interviews with former BR employees.

Although Mike Carruthers of Fairhurst's suggested the problem of water penetration had been identified as early as 1934, Ribblehead did not start causing BR major problems until the 1950s and 60s when it was noticed several pier ends were cracking. At that stage the problems were still manageable if increasingly expensive. But then BR succeeded in complicating the issue by making a somewhat open-ended promise to the Department of Transport that once the West Coast main line was electrified the Settle-Carlisle could probably close. This was far from the case: if anything traffic over the route increased after electrification as -- because there were no catch points on the main line -- all the old-style, non-continuously braked freight traffic had to travel via the Settle-Carlisle.

But maintenance had already been cut back because of what had been said to the Department of Transport and when it was proposed in the late 60s the viaduct should be re-waterproofed the scheme was dropped because of lack of finance and paranoia lest the DTp's "spies" should find out. But major repairs were becoming increasingly urgent and, as bricks began falling from beneath the arches, it was decided to reline some of them. This necessitated single line working and because there were no cross-over points between Horton and Blea Moor it meant single-line working for some six miles. To have installed a new set of points at Ribblehead would have meant resignalling Blea Moor. The budget resources were not available to do this without the BR board being made aware, a prospect which was considered undesirable as the work would be construed by the DTp as "investment".

But the traffic was simply too great to contemplate doing the work in summer and so repairs were carried out in winter when the extreme weather -- which can be evil at Ribblehead even in summer -- cut productivity by something like 50 per cent. BR's spending of £100,000 a year on Ribblehead maintenance between 1974 and 1984 should be seen in this context. After about £250,000 had been spent relining arches it began to be appreciated the extent to which this was really only attacking an effect rather than the cause of Ribblehead's problems. The London-Midland's bridges and structures engineer Frank Leeming (who was, incidentally, on a personal level a great fan of the Settle-Carlisle) believed the solution lay in building a new viaduct. That was not a decision taken lightly: it should be seen first of all in the context of an engineering climate in which repairing structures was becoming more expensive due to higher labour costs while the price of new structures was falling due to lower manufacturing costs. Mr Leeming was possibly a little ahead of his time, but it should also be remembered that while building bridges is something engineers know all about, repairing them often involves dealing with unknowns. It seems Ribblehead epitomised the problem.

Meanwhile, it must be remembered that no-one was proposing the closure of the Settle-Carlisle at this time -- as far as Mr Leeming was concerned he was recommending action to ensure the continued running of a railway with an indefinite life to take 25-ton axle-load freight trains at 70 mph and passenger trains at 90 mph. A variety of options for Ribblehead were considered and approaches were made to a number of major contractors for their ideas for repairing the viaduct. It became clear that none of them were keen to tackle the work as specified because they submitted high estimates with no guarantees as to the effectiveness or otherwise of the remedial work. At the root of the problem was the fact that no-one knew for certain the exact mechanism of failure of the viaduct beyond the obvious fact that water penetration was playing a major role. Other options were considered -- casing the entire structure in concrete was dismissed as unsightly and too costly, while BR's Derby research laboratories concluded that replacing the viaduct with an embankment could result in trains blowing off the track (a conclusion the Midland Railway engineers had come to more than 100 years previously). In short, everything pointed towards Mr Leeming's rebuild option at a cost of £4.5m.

The reconstruction option was not one considered lightly but, as Mr Leeming himself (now retired, in line with BR policy to do away with specialist bridge engineers) recalled: "We were looking towards a continuing railway -- my job was to inform my management what the situation was for a continuing railway and we decided reconstruction was the most economic in the long term. We tried all sorts of schemes but the soundest was to replace it -- when you start tarting up old structures you don't know what you are getting.

"We knew what the problem was but nobody will ever believe the professional," said Mr Leeming. "It was age -- I am still of the opinion that if you want the line there for another hundred years the scheme put forward by the railways originally is the one to follow. I don't believe there are any techniques for repair work for that particular structure which are valid. It's an open-ended contract as to the amount of money you will pour into that viaduct because you don't know what you are tackling."

Building a new viaduct had other attractions: "One of the main considerations is to interrupt traffic as little as possible -- we could simply build a new viaduct alongside the old one and the original structure could stay if it wants."

This internal London Midland debate was going on at a time when the Government was just beginning to turn the screw on

BR spending. But what really threw the cat among the pigeons, as Mr Leeming put it, was the public revelation of it all in an exclusive in the magazine, Steam World, in April 1981. The subject was the question as to whether BR should undertake a major investment in building a new viaduct, a decision which could only be taken at British Railways Board level. It was a subject the board was presumably not even aware of -- until they read about it in Steam World. But the Steam World article not only set out exactly the options drawn up by the then Divisional Civil Engineer, Alan King -- it also included artist's impressions from Mr Leeming's bridge office at Euston of three alternative designs for a new viaduct. Steam World commented: "This is a subject on which BR officials will say nothing at the moment, but it is reasonable to assume that refusal of funds for the new Ribblehead Viaduct will result in the closure of the Settle & Carlisle as a through route."

The Steam World scoop appeared to represent a "leak" of exceptional proportions, yet from the fact that Mr King was later elevated to Assistant Regional Civil Engineer for the London Midland Region it can only be assumed that any part he may have played in it was not considered reprehensible. It can be summised that the immediate effect of the leak, once the shock had worn off, would be to leave the BR board quite gleeful: here was a ready-made pretext on which to lose 72 remote route-miles at a stroke and nobody would be greatly upset. The latter assumption -- and it certainly was a widely held one within BR -- was of course to prove very wide of the mark.

The track mileage problem was also very much a London Midland one -- while other regions had been carrying out a steady rationalisation programme, the London Midland seemed to be plagued by problems which prevented easy solutions to complex track patterns. At a time when most of its resources were going into the West Coast electrification programme, the region had still not come to grips with its excess track mileage. Closing the Settle-Carlisle could be an easy alternative to "more sensible" rationalisation. By contrast, other regions had gone a long way towards solving their problems -- the Eastern, for example, had achieved considerable savings by closing the

Woodhead freight route.

Of course once the fuss caused by publication began to subside a little, people began to look round for a scapegoat -- as usual it was the poor old engineer. Frank Leeming had already been associated with the problems of the Barmouth viaduct which threatened to close the Cambrian Coast line and, as he put it, "my name has been bandied about for various reasons". "People seem to forget that we were professional railway bridge engineers -- I had been in that job all my life, unlike a lot of people who come along and they may be civil engineers, but they are not used to maintaining structures." As Settle-Carlisle Project Manager Ron Cotton put it to me: "As far as the engineers are concerned it's very much a subjective judgement and you do get different views from people equally well qualified on the same problem. What you have got fundamentally, underneath, is a quite justifiable fear that if anything did happen they carry the can ultimately -- you may well say that there is a certain erring on the side of safety." It is certainly the view of the author that the knee-jerk reaction of people in assuming that engineers are persuaded to compromise their professional integrity by saying whatever BR wants them to is totally wrong. Indeed, there have been careers ruined because engineers were judged not to have been careful **enough**. That is not to say, however, that the work of the engineer "on the ground" could be used (misrepresented even) for political ends by others higher up the organisational tree.

More than two years have passed at the time of writing since the Settle-Carlisle closure plan was announced. Ribblehead viaduct -- its track recently singled in line with the Fairhurst recommendation in the PEIDA report -- is still standing and may well count among its blessings two relatively mild Pennine winters and the fact that it is no longer subjected to regular 25-ton axle loads. The financial climate has also changed and it is probably sensible to assume that if the line does not close Ribblehead viaduct is much more likely to be repaired than replaced. There remains, however, a fairly large difference of professional opinion both as to the likely cost of such repairs and to the additional life they might give.

W. A. Fairhurst and Partners compiled their report on the basis of physical inspections of the viaduct after which they then checked their own observations against BR records which gave the exact dates on which particular defects were seen to appear. The company has considerable experience of working both with railway bridges (it was involved in bridgework on the West Coast main line during electrification) and with ageing masonry in the refurbishment of buildings. It summarised its main findings as follows. The technical terms used are explained in the diagram.

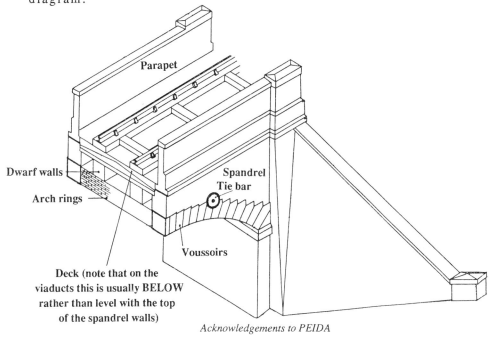

Acknowledgements to PEIDA

☐ Disintegration of the limestone blocks, this being worst at the pier corners.

☐ Separation of the spandrel walls from the arch rings which also allows water to penetrate the piers and arches.

☐ Cracking of the arch rings beneath the internal dwarf walls which carry the track ballast (most of the outer arch rings had already been relined at the time of inspection).

☐ Leaning and misalignment of the parapet walls.

The Fairhurst survey suggested the viaduct's deterioration was accelerating to such an extent that in five years' time repair might no longer be a viable option. The company suggested that to secure the life of the viaduct for 15 years would demand an immediate £2.1m. two-year programme followed by another £0.44m. worth of work over the next 13 years. At that point, it predicted, repairs would again begin to mount significantly -- in years 16 to 20 they could be expected to total about the same as for the previous 15 years (all 1984 prices). The work would include grouting, drilling and stitching the masonry and filling between the spandrel walls with concrete. Alternatively, new waterproofed reinforced concrete decks could be installed beneath the ballast. The original BR estimate for repair had been £4.26m. and Fairhurst's put the difference down to singling and centralising the track over the viaduct so as to improve safety tolerances (it would be supported on the internal walls in the event of a spandrel failure) and thereby reduce the amount that would need to be spent on the parapets and spandrels.

In the light of more optimistic contributions to the debate I asked Fairhurst's partner Mike Carruthers, who carried out the survey work, whether 15-20 years' life was an unduly pessimistic forecast. "An awful lot of stone work now has deteriorated and with the best will in the world you are never going to get back into the situation where they [the viaducts] have another 100 years in front of them," he said. "It's like patching anything up -- you will always have the uncertainty." And he stressed one of the major factors inflating the cost was the weather and the inaccessibility of Ribblehead, which cut not only the number of months in which work was possible but the number of days in those months and the number of hours in those days.

While Mr Leeming's comment on the Fairhurst estimate was "I don't think £2m. is enough but if you are trying to keep it for ten years it probably will", another former BR engineer was convinced that not only could the repairs be carried out for far less, but they would also last pretty well indefinitely.

Chris Wallis is what you might call an innovative engineer by blood -- his father Barnes Wallis conceived the famous

"Dambusters" bouncing bomb and "swing-wing" aircraft among other things. Wallis junior had been in timber research and a private sector bridge engineer until he decided to join BR in 1967, partly out of an ideological belief in public transport. His BR career ended in 1981 after he indulged in bit of "whistle-blowing" over the threat to the Cambrian coast line posed by the need for repairs to a wooden viaduct at Barmouth.

Mr Wallis was angry at what he considered the artificially high price of repairs, with complete replacement mooted among alternatives. Curiously enough, the engineer in charge was one Frank Leeming. Mr Wallis conducted his own, unauthorised, survey and gave it to his superiors in the Western Region on which he was employed (Barmouth was in London Midland). When his more optimistic assessment, as a timber engineer, of the problem did not appear to be being taken notice of, Mr Wallis leaked his report to the Press via the Cambrian Coast Line Action Group. Although much of the work eventually done on the viaduct was broadly in line with his recommendations, Mr Wallis was demoted several grades from management grade two to draughtsman. Although union representation achieved his reinstatement to management grade one, Mr Wallis decided to leave and now runs his own business restoring old buildings (Paul McCartney's windmill is among his more recent contracts).

While with BR, he had devised an original method of repairing the old wooden Loughor viaduct which stands in fast-flowing water near Swansea. His estimate for the job was £295,000 and the actual cost was £293,000. His comment when questioned as to the accuracy of his £0.5m. estimate for repairs to Ribblehead viaduct was: "I would rather have winter than water to contend with."

Fundamental to Mr Wallis's Ribblehead estimate -- compiled on the basis of his own observations -- is that the visible damage to the viaduct is not necessarily as significant structurally as might be supposed. For example, he puts the splitting of the brick arches from the limestone spandrels down primarily to the difficulty of bonding small bricks on to large limestone blocks rather than to any difference in "stiffness" between the two materials. On viaducts where stone was used in both the spandrels and the arch rings the bond was more effective. He also argues that the failure of the outer brick lining ring is unlikely to herald failure of the other five rings. Being nearer the surface and having "more erratic" mortar, left the outer ring more susceptible to weathering and this often peeled off. "It has happened under many arches all over Britain without severe detriment to the structures. The idea that the re-laying of the bottom ring heralds the imminent collapse of the bridge is merely a human reaction," he says.

He further argues that the load from trains does not impose any horizontal force which would tend to push the spandrel walls away from the arches. On the question of the piers themselves, Mr Wallis calculates their ultimate strength at nine tons per square inch whereas their actual load is 0.045 tons per square inch. "Hence small vertical cracks are insignificant," he argues. Mr Wallis's estimate for repairs includes filling the piers themselves, as well as the spandrels, with concrete up to deck level; waterproofing and relaying both tracks on new ballast; pointing and grouting the piers with grout and resin. He believes the existing ties installed to be sufficient.

Other engineers approached by the author disagree with some of Mr Wallis's assertions, particularly as to the lateral forces likely to be exerted on the spandrel walls. It is perhaps worth mentioning that consultants in Scotland have recently drawn up plans for refurbishing for pedestrian traffic only a **disused** viaduct near Kelso at a cost not dissimilar to Mr Wallis's estimate.

The whole Ribblehead question should be seen in the context of other recent railway engineering repair projects. The cost of these ranges from tens or hundreds of thousands of pounds, as in the case of the Durham viaduct on the East Coast and the Lune viaduct on West Coast main lines, to what may be presumed to be the odd million or two for viaducts like Marsh Lane in Leeds or the old Great Northern viaduct in Wakefield, on both of which continual work has been observed for ten years or more. The £1.2m. realignment of the East Coast line where it was slipping into the sea at Burnmouth swallowed a large proportion of the Scottish Region's repair budget in 1983, amid very little publicity. Projects in the pipeline include the closure for waterproofing of at least one main line viaduct, while on the West Coast main line, the price of electrification "on the cheap" without the installation of new ballast and sleepers suitable for high speed running has necessitated a massive ongoing replacement programme.

Nonetheless, there is some question as to whether BR's annual budget provision for bridge repairs actually gets spent. This was a question being pursued in the Commons by Keighley MP Bob Cryer before he lost his seat. Moving to the ridiculous, two enthusiasts' railways in the south of England -- the Romney Hythe and Dymchurch and the Bluebell -- announced investment plans totalling £5m. late in 1985....enough to buy a new Ribblehead viaduct.

Finally, much has been said about the idea that BR should seek finance for Settle-Carlisle from the Common Market or from the Historic Buildings Commission. In the former case a problem lies in the fact that the line does not lie in an "Assisted Area", although an application for funds is being discussed at the time of writing by nearby Bradford Metropolitan district which is an intermediate area. To qualify for grant it would have to be argued that the work was either of broad EEC interest, strategic importance or likely to give substantial benefit to an assisted area (Bradford). There is a firm view among its EEC partners that Britain should pay for its own railway **repairs**, as distinct from investment. PEIDA considered EEC funding "unlikely".

Ribblehead viaduct, as an officially designated Ancient Monument, could well attract some grant aid for repair. PEIDA put the figure at between £0.2m. and £0.5m. It also estimated that between £1.4m. and £4.2m. could be raised through various bodies and through subscriptions and share issues, for repairs on the line as a whole.

Lord Nelson crosses Arten Gill viaduct in February 1984. Picture by Ian Jopson

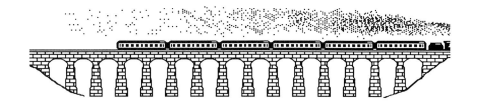

7. Haven't I heard that somewhere before?

PSSST!! Have you heard the one about the line British Rail tried to close because a bridge was falling down?...."Oh, that's an old one!" The story is indeed almost as old as the railways themselves. When private profit was the only consideration lines often closed because the cost of, say, repairing a flood-damaged bridge on a lightly used branch line was simply not justifiable. But under the 1962 Act, the likely cost of any capital works needed on a line ought not, theoretically, be a consideration in the public proceedings to close it.

In practice this is not quite the way things happen -- the Settle-Carlisle case is by no means the first closure proposal in which the ugly spectre of a damning engineer's report hangs menacingly backstage. Given current Government policy it is unlikely to be the last. The scenario builds up something like this:

☐ A series of leaks casts doubts about the general viability of the line from A to C.

☐ BR retimes trains so they miss their connections but repeatedly denies any plans to close the line.

☐ Meanwhile, journalists are told a major study is underway into the cost of repairs to a viaduct across a river at B.

☐ BR engineers complete their work and draw up a list of options involving the expenditure of varying amounts of money to assure various desired lifespans.

☐ The options find their way to the Press which then proceeds to do BR's job for it by highlighting the most costly option, which then becomes in all future articles "the £x m. cost of saving the A-C railway".

☐ BR issues a closure notice for the line and the TUCC

hearings go ahead in an atmosphere prejudiced by Press coverage which has told only part of the story.

The Cambrian Coast line mentioned in the last chapter is one quite famous example of this embellished version of the simple "closure by stealth" process. Closure scares were nothing new to this spectacular line which runs from the Aberystwyth line near Machynlleth 45 miles round the coast to Pwllheli -- the Cambrian Coast Line Action Group was formed in response to the threat to the line in the 1971 which was only lifted in 1974. Some of the line's running costs as quoted by BR at the time have that old ring of familiarity about them....in 1971, for example, the line's signalling costs were put at £68,000 -- by 1973, despite the closure of one signal box, the figure had risen to £112,000. In 1968, BR threatened to close the footpath over the Barmouth viaduct as it was said to need £850-worth of repairs that year and another £3,400 by 1970. After some wrangling Meirionydd County Council leased the footbridge from BR, completed all the necessary repairs for £260 and made a profit on tolls of £216 in the first year.

Despite the general scepticism such experience created, the action group remained willing initially to accept at face value BR's announcement in September 1980 (at a press conference which followed much leaking) that it would have to close the wooden viaduct at Barmouth the following month while a survey was carried out to determine the extent of repairs needed due to worm damage to the wooden piles. By January BR was saying its worst fears had been realised and its initial repair estimate of £2.5m. was about right. The engineer in charge was Frank Leeming who, as already stated, was later to find himself playing a not dissimilar role on the Settle-Carlisle. Among options costed was a replacement viaduct, but a £155,000 survey suggested repair might be possible using one of two alternative methods.

The whole debate was taking place in a highly charged political atmosphere in which no secret was made of the fact that BR was using the Barmouth viaduct as a stick with which to beat more money out of the Government. The then BR Chairman, Sir Peter Parker, had told the Cardiff Business Club the previous November that it was impossible to "continue to deliver indefinitely a fixed contract for a declining sum of money", namely to continue running rural railways while the Government kept cutting the Public Service Obligation grant. Sir Peter was even pictured on TV on Barmouth viaduct wielding a piece of worm-ridden timber which had allegedly been taken from the viaduct. The London Midland's divisional passenger manager at Stoke-on-Trent told a public meeting at Barmouth that BR was using the viaduct as an issue so it could achieve a broader agreement with the Government on funding for railways in general and rural ones in particular. "If we can't get a deal for Barmouth viaduct then we can't get a deal for other lines," he said.

On the face of it, then, BR and the action group were on the same side...or were they? There was a very real fear among the action group's members that the Government would simply "call BR's bluff", whereupon BR would either close the line or lose a lot of face. The group's May 1981 bulletin put it this way: "BR -- at the highest level -- may well be prepared to sacrifice the Cambrian line on the well known and much frequented altar of political expediency; to prove a point to the Government and as a dramatic gesture to 'prove' what they're saying about rural railways."

Then the Cambrian would become just another rural railway closed for want of capital to make repairs, and the sideline of BR's battle with the Government would be irrelevant history for the people affected. But BR's Government-bashing cudgel suddenly began to look a little limp when Chris Wallis, as described in the previous chapter, gave the action group a copy of his report suggesting the viaduct could be satisfactorily repaired for just a tenth the £2.5m. figure claimed by BR. He had been driven to leak his report by the apparent reluctance of BR to act on it.

Mr Wallis's main finding was that the damage was far less severe than BR had been saying. He claimed that only about ten per cent of the timber piles had been mildly attacked by shipworm -- they had all been attacked by gribble worm, which was less serious, causing only surface damage. The rotten timber wielded by Sir Peter had, it seems, come from the remains of the previous viaduct demolished at the start of the century. He also criticised the manner in which previous repairs had been carried out, claiming some were actually more likely to cause further damage. Drawing on his experience in repairing the Loughor viaduct, Mr Wallis proposed what he called a "simple, foolproof and lasting repair".

The immediate effect of this report, apart from the demotion of Mr Wallis, was a halving of BR's original estimate and a new "ultimatum" to the Government. BR said it was doing repairs which would allow the viaduct to reopen, but only for six months, whereupon if the Government did not provide £1.2m. to complete repair work it would have to close again. The Government did not cough up -- certainly it was not **seen** to cough up. But neither did the viaduct close and by the end of 1985 it was again able to take the full weight of loco-hauled trains. Some piles had been repaired in line with Mr Wallis's suggested method and others had been replaced. BR found the money "from internal sources" and it is not clear whether the Government made any adjustment in the PSO grant to help BR.

The moral of the story would seem to be that if you want to make a political point to the Government you should first make cast-iron sure of your facts. As Chris Wallis put it: "Leeming should have got a good timber engineer like me to come and look at the viaduct in the first place." Mr Leeming for his part stands by his original view, claiming one of the supporting piers was so decayed it was broken by the rowing boat carrying an inspection party. "The railway engineer was doing his job and doing it correctly," he said. The fact that the viaduct was still there now was thanks only to the ability of the engineers to keep it open against the economic odds, he added.

In the 1980 Cambrian Coast closure scare, unlike the previous threat in the 70s, no BR closure notice was ever actually issued. A case in which a railway actually faced official closure proceedings against the background of a major engineering problem, pre-dating the Settle-Carlisle by 15 years, was the Afan Valley line in South Wales. Losing Track, by Hamilton and Potter, tells how some 13,000 people signed a petition objecting to plans to close the line which ran from Treherbert to a summit at

1,500ft., through a tunnel and then to Bridgend. In 1968 the tunnel was declared unsafe for use and closed. A replacement bus service was put on via the mountainous road which climbed to 1,800ft.. It took an hour rather than the ten minutes taken by the train. The cost of repairing the tunnel was estimated at between £20,000 and £30,000 but because the closure notice had been issued, the work was not begun. Despite the obvious value of a speedy link between valleys which were accessible from one another by road only with difficulty, permission was granted for the closure of the line in 1969. The cost of repairs to the tunnel which, Hamilton and Potter comment, "technically should not have been a consideration" was "clearly influential".

Another closure threat row centring on the cost of repairs to a neglected bridge blew up in 1983, back in Yorkshire. This time the route in question was far from being a lightly used rural one -- the Goole-Gilberdyke line is part of the Inter-City route from Hull to King's Cross and is used by about 200,000 passengers a year. Nontheless BR proposed closing it because some £2.2m.-worth of repairs were needed to a swing bridge over the Humber at Goole. Inter-City services would be diverted round two sides of a triangle via Selby, an increasingly important centre on the new coalfield to which it gives its name. The closure notice brought more than 3,000 objections.

The story was in many ways the same old one we have heard before -- the bridge repair bill had steadily mounted over years of neglect. The need for repairs at Goole stemmed from a cause rather different from the ravages of Pennine weather, however. The bridge had been struck by a coaster in December 1973, causing about £1m.-worth of damage, but for legal reasons peculiar to the world of marine insurance, BR's claim yielded only £15,016. Since then, up to January 1985, another 22 ships had collided with the bridge's central jetty, 12 of them causing "more than superficial" damage. There was good reason to believe powerful lobbies outside the railways -- this time representing shipping rather than road interests -- were backing the closure plan to allow access up-river for larger vessels. Humberside county council chiefs visited the bridge with their engineer and pronounced themselves "appalled" at the way in which the bridge had been allowed to deteriorate.

But the fact that it would in any case cost BR £1m. to demolish the bridge if the line closed helped provide the basis for a solution -- the county council offered to put up £400,000 towards the cost of repairs if the line stayed open. The offer was made amid real fear for Hull's London link as diversion via Selby would have entailed using another problem swing bridge. The Selby bridge used also to carry the East Coast main line until the commencement of mining necessitated (or offered an opportunity for) the building of a new line away from the town. Months of bartering saw the local authority offer rise to £1.1m. or 50 per cent of the repair cost. But BR remained determined to press ahead with closure unless it was given this sum "up front".

Eventually BR appeared to relent and a deal was made under which the county council would give BR £800,000 immediately and the balance would be spread over five years as repairs were carried out. In return BR would guarantee the future of the line for ten years. BR also promised Parliamentary action over the outdated marine insurance laws which contributed to the crisis. Critics of the deal believe it is too open-ended and does not tie BR to specific enough undertakings. Certainly BR had every reason to feel very pleased with their bargaining -- if the Clitheroe DalesRail station reopening (Chapter Two) had in its small way set the precedent for securing local authority finance for railway schemes, here was a far more significant attraction of such finance. Goole swing bridge is believed to be the first occasion on which an authority has contributed directly to BR's maintenance budget. The Barmouth scare may have cut little ice with the Government, but Goole had quite spectacular results in attracting funds from a different quarter.

It is too early to judge, as this book is being written, whether the Goole solution is going to precipitate a rash of bridges and viaducts in "imminent danger of collapse" demanding instant injections of scarce local authority funds to stave off railway closures. In November 1985 there was Press speculation that BR was ready to make a similar deal over the Settle-Carlisle, whereby if an outside body was prepared to put up £5m, BR would match the sum and carry out the most urgent repairs. But

BR's Settle-Carlisle Project Manager Ron Cotton denied any suggestion of a pound-for-pound deal. He said the £5m. figure had arisen quite incidentally when he told the Friends of the Settle-Carlisle Line Association that a sum of that order would need to be guaranteed as a prerequisite to any negotiations on the subject. It might nontheless still be thought significant that BR should have gone on record as being prepared even to consider talking about a rescue package on any terms whatsoever, especially one that would involve BR itself in major expenditure.

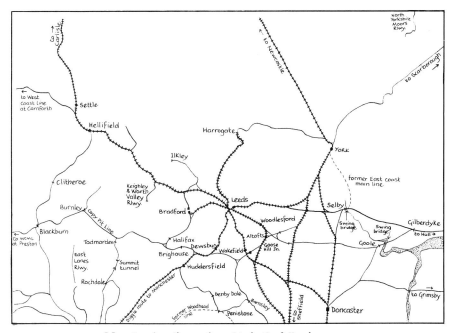

Map showing lines referred to in the following pages

113

A BR-local authority cash wrangle of a rather different kind lay behind another closure threatened at the time of writing. The threat facing the Huddersfield-Denby Dale section of the Huddersfield-Sheffield line revolves around the sticky concept of the "prime user" detailed earlier in this book. British Rail began closure proceedings after West Yorkshire County Council refused to meet BR demands for a £500,000-a-year contribution towards running costs -- compared with £300,000 in 1983. But the council argues that, while the West Yorkshire PTE is the prime user of the section in question, the line also serves as a feeder for Inter-City services from Huddersfield and Sheffield. West Yorkshire's compromise offer of £200,000 proved insufficient to tempt BR back to the negotiating table.

The situation of this line is further complicated by legal questions arising from a 1981 BR attempt to close the Denby Dale to Sheffield section, this time after South Yorkshire County Council refused to pay the contribution demanded by BR. But the line was reprieved when it was agreed to divert the trains on the section south of Penistone, via Barnsley. The move -- involving the reopening for passenger use of a freight-only line -- led to a 50 per cent increase in passengers, with South Yorkshire funding the line as far as Penistone. The short stretch straddling the county boundary between Penistone and Denby Dale is funded by BR which claims it already has Government sanction to close that part of the route by virtue of the 1981 ministerial decision following the TUCC hearings. If the ministerial decision, expected in 1986, were to permit closure it would undoubtedly herald a long legal battle as the Huddersfield-based Kirklees council has pledged to take High Court action to prevent withdrawal of trains between Denby Dale and Penistone. The council is backed by the TUCC for North-East England in its contention that BR can not retain authority for closure indefinitely. The TUCC argues there are many new users of the service since the 1981 closure hearing who have a legal right to object to the closure plan which was denied them at the autumn 1985 hearings.

In December 1984 a question mark suddenly loomed out of the blue over another of West Yorkshire's rail links -- the trans-Pennine line from Bradford to Manchester via Rochdale. The derailment of an oil tanker in the Summit tunnel near Todmorden was followed by a massive blaze which sent flames erupting a hundred feet above the ventilation shafts like a volcano. The theory was that an axle box had overheated on one of the tankers which had been working "overtime" during the miners' strike. There were immediate fears the tunnel had been damaged beyond repair and BR would give no commitment to reopen the line. Prospects looked particularly bleak in that BR had already been searching for economies, including track-singling, and all but one of the Yorkshire stations could be served by the new Leeds to Preston service if the tunnel did close.

In the event, repairs were carried out rather more quickly than at first thought possible and the line reopened. In the current climate of "route rationalisation" it is worth making this a starting point for a speculative exercise on how the rail network in Yorkshire and the North of England generally might be "reshaped" should the current process of attrition continue to be fostered by the Government. In that the tunnel fire might well have handed the closure of this high-maintenance trans-Pennine route to BR on a plate, the question as to why it was decided to retain it needs to be asked. One possible answer lies in its value as a freight route -- the 1965 Trunk Route report (see Chapter Three) preferred it to the more direct Leeds-Manchester Inter-City route via Diggle because the gradients were generally easier. Late in 1985 BR decided to make this its primary trans-Pennine freight route in conjunction with the old Lancashire and Yorkshire line through Brighouse, thereby easing passenger timings via Diggle.

Perhaps more relevant is a possible long-term strategic importance of the Copy Pit route from Leeds to Preston. Track from just west of Halifax as far as Todmorden is common to both routes. Internal London Midland sources have indicated that it was intended to close the Copy Pit route on which the Freight Sector was the sole user. Freight services had largely been diverted along other paths when a decision was suddenly taken to retain the line and reopen it to passenger services. The new

Leeds-Preston service started in October 1984.

The Association of Metropolitan Authorities/Association of County Councils Councils' joint Statement of Concern to the Secretary of State for Transport in 1985 (see Chapter Five) drew attention to the problem of the reallocation of costs when Inter-City and freight services were withdrawn from a route, as in the case of the Settle-Carlisle. "It has been suggested that the removal [.....] would mean that the Aire Valley line costs would be borne entirely by the remaining Public Service Obligation service and the Passenger Transport Executive's Section 20 services. The argument goes that if the Carnforth service then proved to be untenable, all route costs would fall on the Leeds/Bradford to Skipton and Ilkley services. This could give rise to the PTE finding that the level of support was unattractive and seeking to withdraw both these services."

This is the rail closure "domino effect" theory in a nutshell -- that far from making the alternative Leeds-Carlisle route via Carnforth more secure, closure of the Settle-Carlisle could actually make it more vulnerable. The original "Heads of Information" document sent to objectors said the proposed alternative Leeds-Carlisle service via Carnforth and the West Coast main line would add about 15 to 20 minutes to existing journey times by the direct route (over which timings were in any case considerably slower than they had been). The revised Heads of Information issued in December 1985 said this difference would in fact be about 30 minutes. Settle-Carlisle Project Manager Ron Cotton said this increase had been due to difficulty obtaining paths over the West Coast line for the new service.

It does not take a genius to work out that this timing would then be quite close to the sort of timing that could be achieved by running the service via Copy Pit and Preston, thereby taking in a far more heavily populated catchment area and opening the door to closure of the line between Settle Junction and Carnforth. The service could even be routed via Brighouse to improve timings. The argument cuts the other way too -- if the Settle-Carlisle is retained, the London Midland may then find itself looking for alternative route mileage savings and the

Carnforth line could again become a candidate. BR's stock comment to questions about the future of the Carnforth line is that it has "no plans" to seek its closure. But then BR had "no plans" to close the Settle-Carlisle either.

It is worth speculating which other lines might be at risk from the domino effect, should the current Government's policy of refusing BR enough money to run a railway continue. Strictures on the spending of the metropolitan counties and the uncertainty as to the functioning of the Joint Boards due to replace them in April 1986, makes some of the more lightly used PTE lines obvious candidates -- when the transport authorities find themselves bearing all the overheads of lines and facing continued cash cuts the superficial arguments for bus substitution become very persuasive. A Yorkshire Post report in October 1985 identified West Yorkshire's most vulnerable services as Leeds and Bradford to Ilkley, Bradford to Keighley and Huddersfield to Wakefield. The Leeds-Castleford-Pontefract-Goole line has been mentioned as another vulnerable route, but the decision to repair Goole swing bridge could raise another possibility. If BR was looking at the problem in trunk traffic terms, an attractive option for a Humber-Mersey route might be via Goole, thereby adding the Calder towns to the catchment area. Current through routeings are via Doncaster, although better timings are available by changing at Leeds on the "old" through route.

The Leeds route via Selby involves the use of the "problem" swing bridge there and plans were mooted in 1985 for single line working between Gilberdyke junction and the junction with the Leeds-York line at Micklefield. Severing the Hull line east of Selby might have appeal for Eastern Region as an alternative to Goole-Gilberdyke closure but might necessitate the retention of the direct Leeds-Castleford line to give reasonable timings. (At the time of writing it is planned to close this line and its two stations and route all trains via Wakefield to give the Calder towns a better InterCity link.)

The willingness of the London Midland to sacrifice its Settle-Carlisle diversionary route after the West Coast electrification programme must prompt conjecture as to whether the Eastern Region might consider doing the same with its diversionary routes during the coming electrification programme, such as those avoiding Darlington and Durham. The foregoing closure possibilities are purely speculative and it is certainly to be hoped they do not give BR any ideas that have not occurred already!

Finally, as an aside to the "closure by stealth" argument, it is worth quoting the findings of Mayer Hillman and Anne Whalley in their research on the consequence of rail closures for the Policy Studies Institute (also mentioned in Chapter Six). Their 1978 survey work in ten areas which had lost their rail links suggested that allegations that BR had deliberately discouraged the use of routes which it wished to close were not reflected in the passenger census figures for those routes. In fact the rate of decline in use of those lines was actually slower than on the railway system at large. Some of the study's other findings are considered later.

Jack Sedgwick, the last signalman at the now closed Dent box.
Picture by John and Eliza Forder.

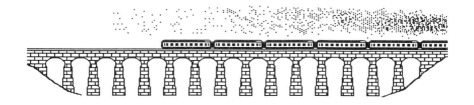

8. Railway people

A FRESH sou'westerly was blowing the weather straight up the
dale off the Irish sea as Neville Caygill swung off the road by the
old Station Inn beneath Ribblehead viaduct's protective bulk.
Pulling on wellies and waterproofs, Neville turned his back on
the wind and rain and prepared for work. For work for this
46-year-old father-of-two begins with a mile-and-a-half's trek
across windswept moorland.

Blea Moor -- the very name rings with desolation. But its
signal box was, by 1985, the only permanently manned one
between Settle, 12 miles to the south, and Kirkby Stephen, 18
miles north. At 1,100ft. above sea level it can lay claim to being
the highest and most remote box on the BR network. Neville
works the box alternate shifts with his mate Mick from Horton
-- at six miles it's a shorter drive than Neville faces. Neville lives
just eight miles down the line from Blea Moor at the Moorcock
railway cottages, but it's 15 wild miles whichever road you take.

But things could have been a lot worse as Neville slung his
havversack across his shoulder and strode off towards the great
arches, leaving me struggling to catch up. For a start it could
have been a 5 a.m. start and dark instead of two in the
afternoon. It could, for that matter, have been a "real" winter
instead of the mild and damp half-winter we had in the Dales in
late 1984. "If the road's blocked I have to ring Skipton and tell
them I can't get," said Neville. "Then they have to either find a
train to pick me up or send somebody else from down their way
-- but there's usually a snowplough comes through early from
Carlisle and they'll stop at Garsdale for me." Worse for Neville is
when the weather comes in bad while he's at work: "There's

times when I've had to drive right round by Ingleton and Sedbergh, and that's about 33 miles."

Neville came to Blea Moor after working the Dent box, now closed, as is Horton since the Union of South Africa started a lineside fire which burnt out the cables. Garsdale is the only other box kept in working order and manned occasionally when traffic demands. Blea Moor used to be an important spot in the Settle-Carlisle's heyday, marking the end of the Long Drag up from Settle. Today just one of the old tunnel gang's cottages remains, belonging to a school in Liverpool whose pupils make only occasional visits. Neville's job now is to look after the points at the Ribblehead ballast sidings the other end of the viaduct as well as the cross-over points and the old passing loops at Blea Moor itself.

The first job on a morning is to switch the points for the early train from Settle to Leeds...yes, Settle to Leeds. This diesel multiple unit runs 30 miles empty from Skipton to Blea Moor every day just to turn round. It then runs 15 miles back to Settle, still empty, where it then starts its days work. To have installed cross-over points nearer Settle would, of course, have been "investment", so 14,000 wasted train miles go on the bill for running the line instead -- that's equivalent to more than half way round the world! To say the train runs empty, however, is not strictly correct -- it drops off two containers of drinking water for the signalmen every day. "It must be the dearest drinking water in the country," said Neville. "If they gave us in money what it costs to bring water up every day I'd carry the bugger from Ribblehead myself!"

The Blea Moor box used to have its own water supply until about ten years ago when a derailed goods train sliced through the pipe. In fact you could call Blea Moor the "used to" signal box. There used to be a cabin for train crews to spend the night in the days when Blea Moor was a change-over point. There used to be 20 trains go through in a shift even by Neville's recent memory. There used to be a coal-fired stove to warm the box against the fierce elements....but that had gone a few weeks earlier, explained Neville as we ended our trek to relieve Mick. Mick it was who had tried to coax a bit more heat from the lousy coal only for the stove to go up in flames. The firemen had to carry their pump a mile along the track to douse the blaze with water from a bog.

The steady plip-plop-plip as buckets gathered drips beneath the holes where the firemen ripped the slates from the roof, filled the lonely box with an earie music. But this was to be a very unusual day at Blea Moor -- Neville had not just one but three visitors. Toby the technician from Settle and his mate were busy warming themselves by the temporary Calor gas fire after making a few routine repairs. Calor gas also runs the lights and the cooker in the box -- the only electricity is the low-current 240-volt supply which runs Toby's signalling equipment. "Toby says we can't use his electricity to run a light," complained Neville.

Outside the box a stoat scurried in the rubble as Neville pulled out the bird-watching book the men bought as a bright idea for passing the hours -- but the hawks never seem to come close enough. "There are a few herons around the beck though," said Neville. The departure of Toby and mate gave Neville the chance to reflect again on the loneliness. "Sometimes I'm glad to get away from it," he said. "You can't fall out with anybody when you're on your own." And then again he was thankful just to have a job: "Last year at this time I didn't expect to be here now, but we've got another year so you never know.

Neville Caygill at Blea Moor signal box. Northern Echo picture.

"But the job's no good as it is -- yesterday I didn't even see a train from two til five. There's no interest in it any more and it's been going on so long   no-one has any interest in the job any more."

Working becomes more a question of passing the time at Blea Moor -- radio is not allowed so Neville romps through all the Dick Francis and Dennis Wheatley books his wife Sylvia can lay hands on at the little library at Hawes. The rain rattled the windows and the wind whistled under the eaves, as dusk signalled time to fight my way back across the moor into the face of the weather.

Since that interview a year has passed and in 1986 Neville faces his busiest spell at work for some time. It will be another summer that could be the last on the line and at the time of writing BR was already reckoning on extra scheduled trains to meet demand, not to mention the steam-hauled and other special excursions. Neville told me then not one of his railway colleagues in the Hawes area thought closure would be anything but a matter of time. Today people aren't so sure. Even BR management admit the decision could go either way if it even comes at all this side of a General Election. Neville, with a son and daughter at school in Hawes and Leyburn is one of many awaiting closure with some trepidation, having lived most of his life in the area. The only consolation of moving to another BR region might be the chance to actually be near enough a working station to make use of his quota of travel passes!

For a community which lost its own station a quarter of a century ago, Hawes retains a surprisingly strong railway allegiance which is not immediately apparent to the hordes of summer visitors to this predominantly agricultural Dales market town. In fact, after Appleby, Hawes arguably stands to lose most should the Settle-Carlisle close. When the closure threat first loomed in the early 80s there were about 20 people in the town and its satellite villages. Some with strong ties to the area have since left when other jobs have come up locally, while a few have "followed the railway" and taken work in other parts of the country. But even at only about 15 jobs, British Rail can still claim joint second place (with the ropeworks) in the area's employment stakes, after the Milk Marketing Board creamery which provides work for about 100. And if the line should close, then, as Neville put it "that's a lot of jobs to find for a place the size of Hawes". For even if all 15 chose to take whatever alternative employment BR offered (wherever it might be) under union agreements, it would still represent a loss of opportunities and a further constriction of the narrow economic base of an area which is increasingly dependent on the highly seasonal tourist trade to supplement the traditional sheep and dairy farming and their associated service industries.

Apart from the signalmen, the railway workers at Hawes are the rump of the maintenance gangs which not long ago totalled nearly 100 men on the Kirkby Stephen section, from just north of Settle to just south of Appleby. Today two track gangs operate out of Hawes -- seven "clock on" at Garsdale, six miles west of the town, and six at Ribblehead, ten miles to the south-west. In practice, as the drivers in both gangs live at Gayle just outside Hawes, the men effectively start their day's work by joining the van in time to be at the railway for 7.30. But although the two vans are parked overnight just yards from each other, they fall under different administrative areas and when they are due for their monthly maintenance, one has to be driven 15 miles to Kirkby Stephen and the other 30 miles to Lancaster. It is just another minor aside to the story of missed economies which a closer inspection of the working of the railway reveals.

The Ribblehead gang looks after the stretch from just south of Horton-in-Ribblesdale to Blea Moor, while the Garsdale gang is responsible for the track between Blea Moor and Lunds, near the summit at Aisgill. The men are given their work on a computer schedule from Crewe, but winter on the Settle-Carlisle can see that cast aside, as lengthman Eric Allen explained. "When we have to go icing we don't work to the sheet." Icing means removing the icicles which accumulate overnight in the three tunnels on the gang's patch -- Blea Moor, Rise Hill and Moorcock -- and beneath the Blea Moor aqueduct. "In a right severe frost they can be about the height of this spot," said Eric, indicating vaguely the ceiling of the bar at the Crown Hotel, Hawes. "If you don't keep on top and remove them each day they build up until they're impossible to shift." That's a fact that's easily appreciated when you remember that the water tends these days to pour down the ventilation shafts, the deepest of which has something like a 500ft. drop into Blea Moor tunnel. The men use cut saplings to reach the tunnel roofs to do the job.

Out in the daylight, Eric said the men had replaced something like 1,000 sleepers on the line between Garsdale and Lazonby, which he reckoned put the Settle-Carlisle in a better position in that respect than the West Coast route (see Chapter Seven). Come the 1986 public hearings, Eric will be into his 14th year on the railway since becoming a probationary railwayman at 18. "Most of our gang have been on 30 odd years," he said. He thought he and the other Hawes men, many of whom have families to keep, would now stay with the job until the line's fate was settled one way or the other. And he was quite clear where that fate would ultimately be decided: "The railway isn't run by railwaymen -- it's run by Maggie, whatever anybody says."

Twenty miles up the line at Appleby works another man who, like Eric, will probably choose to follow the work and leave the area if the railway closes. But unlike Eric, Leading Railwayman Paul Holden was not born and bred in the area. "I was manager of a Berni Inn in Bristol but I got fed up and decided to 'drop out' for want of a better word," said Paul. "I have always been a railway enthusiast, so I wrote to British Rail at Carlisle to ask if there wer any jobs."

Paul Holden

The result was six weeks training at Manchester, after which he became signalman at Appleby. "It was a bit busier then, in 1978/79, but when it got so a morning shift was just three trains it was rather monotonous." So when the chance came of becoming "stationmaster" Paul took it. "I get to meet people and go and do the signal lamps and so on," he said.

Under Paul's guidance, Appleby is far from having the neglected, run-down look you might expect of a station on a doomed line. Like Settle, it has a tradition of winning awards for its presentation, although BR did its best to thwart such incentives for improving the quality of travel for passengers when it temporarily banned Appleby from entering the best kept station competition on the grounds that it was due for closure. Paul, now in his late 30s, does not relish the thought of Appleby without its railway. "I don't think I would stay here," he said. "If and when the railway goes I think it will make a big difference to the way of life here and, emotionally, I won't want to stay here when there's no through Settle-Carlisle line.

It is at Appleby, once the proud county town of what used to be Westmorland, that the TUCCs can expect to encounter the greatest number of cases of classic "hardship", for even in its skeletal residual form, the train service remains a lifeline for many. The sense of isolation for this town -- famous for its annual gipsy horse fair -- was increased dramatically in 1985 when the Ribble bus service to Penrith was slashed from between three and five buses daily to and from Penrith to just two a week (at the same time as Kirkby Stephen lost its buses all together). The timing of trains since the withdrawal of InterCity services means their use has become limited by practical considerations to a limited range of journeys. Daily trips to work are impossible and shopping outings to Leeds, for example, are difficult because the schedule allows only two-and-a-half hours there.

But loss of the service would make any southward journeys at all from Appleby a major expedition. For people like 78-year-old Ena Wills the effect would be quite devastating as the train represents her means of seeing her only living relatives, cousins at Keighley and Leeds. "If it comes off, I don't whatever I'm going to do, because Pat and I will never be able to meet," she said. Although she owns a car and drives, the prospect of driving all the way to Leeds is one she can not consider at her age. Besides, why should she drive when her Senior Citizen's Railcard entitles to half price on the train? "There are a lot of us do it," she said. "The effect on Appleby if it goes will be disastrous -- you don't miss the water until the well runs dry. When the weather's bad you just pop on the train: people don't realise how much they use the train until it's gone....they are very apathetic."

Prominent among those fighting to retain the line has been Vanda Braid who moved to Appleby when she and her husband were made redundant five years ago. "Living in Appleby, if you work outside the town, you need a car because there is no transport to get anywhere." As her husband needs the car to drive to work in Penrith, the train gives her and two teenage sons the only chance of mobility. "I use it to go shopping in Leeds and Skipton, but I'd like to see the train back on the old timings because the time it gives in Leeds may be all right for me on my own but if I go with someone else there's just not long enough. You know what it's like when two women get at it!" The train is important for her sons too, giving them the chance to get to Carlisle for concerts (providing they can stay there overnight with friends). "There's not much for young people to do in Appleby unless they are sport orientated," said Vanda. The train service is also well used by young people returning from college at Carlisle for the weekend.

At the other end of line it is, at the time of writing, still possible to commute by train. It is presumed by BR that the existing users will readily transfer their allegiance to the Leeds-Carnforth line which has a pay-train halt called Giggleswick which is actually rather nearer to Settle than to the village which gives it its name. It is a convenient presumption which attaches no value to the amenity of a town centre station with well-kept facilities as opposed to a draughty platform in the middle of nowhere a mile from the town. For people like teacher Peter Lawrence it offers no choice: "I will have to leave home an hour earlier and travel on the bus. It will cause me considerable difficulties, and the same coming home again." He works at Keighley and finds he can use the train journey to get work done. Because working on the bus would be impossible, the loss of the rail service would cost him two hours every day.

The arrival of DalesRail not only gave access to the Yorkshire Dales National Park for city-dwellers -- it renewed the scope for Dalespeople to make journeys which had become impossible with the loss of the local stopping service five years previously. People like Edna Harper who ran the shop at Garsdale Head (once it had also been the Post Office and Miss Harper was a familiar site delivering the mail on her bicycle) could once again take the train and visit her brother in Skipton. Without DalesRail the journey is as good as impossible -- even buses to Hawes run only twice a week. The threatened loss of the service means that people like the elderly Miss Harris are fighting for their lifeline for a third time. But of course the biggest group for whom the legal clarification of the terms of the Transport Act has opened up the scope for objecting comprises the ramblers and others using DalesRail for access to the national park.

The archetypal DalesRail traveller is Graham Nuttall, from Burnley, who with his dog Ruswarp (named after a station on the Whitby line and pronounced Rus'up) has never missed a weekend in the ten years the service has run. Ruswarp, a border collie cross, has the distinction of being the only dog to object the proposed closure, an action he is quite entitled to take under the Transport Act as a fare-paying user of the rail service. "As a teenager I discovered the marvellous access that the former Skipton to Carlisle stopping trains provided into the national park," said Graham.

Graham Nuttall and Ruswarp at Garsdale Station

"I used them every weekend for almost two years with my then dog Chummy until the service closed." Graham was devastated by the loss of the trains which had always been well patronised at weekends when he used them. He had also struck up a friendship with Miss Harper and visiting her now meant catching the express to Appleby, bus to Kirkby Stephen (which there was in those days) and then walking 11 miles come rain or snow. Sometimes they would have to walk 16 miles to Ingleton instead to catch a bus home from there. "Chummy would try to drag me oin to Garsdale station as usual, but how do you explain to a dog that a wretched, uncaring Minister of Transport has axed the service?"

Chummy lived to see the return of trains to Garsdale in the shape of the ramblers' special in 1974 and of DalesRail proper the following year, before he died aged 17. But Ruswarp has proved as much a train and walking fan as his predecessor and Graham believes he would greatly miss his weekends in the Dales each month.

But Graham's assumption that his cat Tibatha would be equally excited at the prospect of striding the fells with him proved ill-founded. "I was reading about a cat that liked walking and so I went to the pet shop and got a collar and lead. I was going for a week's holiday to Edna's and I got the bus to Skipton and the train to Clapham. We got off the train and the cat had the collar and lead on but it wouldn't walk an inch...and we had 16 miles to go! I ended up carrying it all the way." If the line closed it would mean Graham and Ruswarp would have to walk 16 miles to get to Edna's in winter, or six miles in summer when weekend buses run to Hawes.

A significant question to be asked is whether the closure of the residual rail service at places like Appleby which at the time of writing meets only a limited range of the needs of the population would be a major loss to the place. Research data suggests that, notwithstanding the lamentable quality of service, the effects of closure would be quite considerable, particularly at a place like Appleby which is some distance from the nearest alternative railhead.

Mayer Hillman and Ann Whaley's 1978 research (see also Chapter Seven) looked at ten areas which had lost their rail links, including two other towns in Cumbria -- Alston and Keswick -- and Newtown St. Boswell's on the Waverley route which in many ways is the most comparable recent line closure to the Settle-Carlisle proposal. One of their primary conclusions concerned the inability of bus services to form an adequate replacement for trains -- a conclusion backed by both "objective evidence" and the judgements of the respondents in the surveys which formed the basis for the research. "The consequences which we have identified confirm that many of the fears expressed at the TUCC inquiries about how closure would affect rail users were well-founded, and, indeed, suggest that the fears were not widely enough held. Our findings point strongly to a degree of hardship and inconvenience that does not appear to be widely appreciated by people involved in making decisions affecting rural transport, especially those whose day-to-day work involves them in considering people or problems extending beyond the dommunities directly affected by the closures." They argued that appraisal of the consequences of closure should encompass issues far wider than those defined as relating to hardship to former users -- a call which of course is currently being vigorously pursued by West Yorkshire County Council and other authorities opposing closure of the Settle-Carlisle line.

Mayer and Hillman's survey work also revealed, not surprisingly, that car ownership in areas which had lost their rail link had increased more since closure than in other comparable areas, with some who had bought cars saying that their decision was influenced to a marked degree by the closure. "Moreover, it was held, and our survey findings confirm, that once a car has been acquired, use of public transport slumps, and this is as true of the remaining rail network as it is of the local bus services." The survey work also contained findings which should have merited careful consideration by British Rail. Mayer and Hillman's surveys found that only a third of the former railways' users who used to travel beyond the railhead to make longer journeys on the national network continued to do so after the line closed travelled. While the total loss to BR was not within the scope of the survey work, the researchers suggested "the loss has been substantial relative to the population catchments of the line".

Also outside the scope of their work was the question as to the extent to which loss of the rail service had cost the area dear in terms of future opportunities, such as new industries. In the absence of any direct comparison with "control areas", namely those that had retained their rail links, the question became hypothetical. But the finding that came across strongly was the extent to which the loss of the railway was felt within all sections of the community as creating a deep-seated feeling of isolation, because of the reduced opportunities for travel, which endured for considerable time after the tracks had been lifted.

In winter, road conditions show the value of the railway. Picture by Ian Jopson, with Ribblehead viaduct in the background.

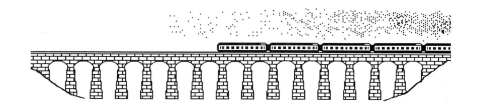

9. Disneyland in the Dales

IF you go up on the fells today you're sure of a big surpise....for every photographer there ever was, will seem to buzzing about there because, today's the day the steam trains are out on the railway!

Those unprepared for the spectacle may well find it difficult to believe their eyes when they witness the quite enormous number of steam train enthusiasts and amateur photographers who will gather in all weathers to snatch a piece of celluloid posterity, courtesy of the Steam Locomotive Operators Association and the Settle-Carlisle railway.

Here at the very heart of the Pennines -- where the rivers Eden, Ure and Clough rise within a few miles of each other and flow respectively north, east and south -- the very names evoke the isolation of the place: Mallerstang Common, Dandry Mire, Hellgill, Hangingstone Scar.

The invasion of the camera gang soon shatters the solitude: vaulting gates and leaping ditches, they come by the hundred -- thousand even -- hell-bent on jostling for the best vantage point. They wait, sometimes for hours, jealously guarding that new camera angle and hoping the beloved iron horse will obligingly belch steam at just the moment to create the classic picture so admired by the connoisseurs.

The moment past, the few precious frames clicked, the madness for some begins. Some even resort to motorcycles in their endeavours to catch another chance of snapping the object of their admiration further up the line. Parish councillors at Hawes have condemned the maniac road-racing which follows the passage of a steam train through Aisgill Summit. Taken at its worst, this increasingly regular pilgrimage of "steam buffs" is an unwelcome intrusion into the lives of the people who farm these lonely hills. The other side of the coin is the extent to which this extraordinary spectacle reflects the strength of the wave of steam-age nostalgia sweeping Britain, and the Settle-Carlisle line in particular.

But the great dilemma is finding a means of translating this fanaticism into pounds and pence to run a railway. It was summed up for me the day we took a 280-mile circular steam-hauled excursion, taking in the Settle and Carlisle. Those on board belonged in roughly equal numbers to three categories -- members and guests of the Darlington section of the Permanent Way Institution; steam fanatics; and members of the general public interested in taking a ride over the Settle-Carlisle. The Institution had organised the trip to mark its centenary and had had little difficulty filling the other 300 seats with only limited advertising, despite the fact it was running on a week-day.

The steam fanatics were characteristically conspicuous by their notebooks, stopwatches and cameras, taking advantage of every watering halt to rush out and take pictures of the ex-Southern Railways locomotive, Sir Lamiel. "I've travelled the line about five or six times so far this year," said one. "If I'm not on a steam special I'm usually taking pictures of it -- I just wish there was some way of converting that photography into cash to keep the trains running." And there lies the catch -- British Rail sees this ostensibly keep-coming-back-for-more market as a very fickle one: "The trouble is that if the steam enthusiasts had to pay the full economic fare they'd be just as happy to go out and take pictures of the trains instead," said BR's InterCity Services Manager David Ward.

The pricing of steam excursions is not straightforward, but in general terms they are subsidised by the locomotives' owners for whom looking after and exercising their pride and joy is a labour of love. The operators pay to charter the train itself -- and the crew -- from BR (limited training of new crews is even taking place). Mr Ward reckons each of the 30 or so steam locomotives touting for excusion business needs to earn about £8,000 a year, but is lucky if it achieves half that figure. "There are far too many engines chasing too little work," he said.

Waiting for the train -- steam
enthusiasts pictured by Ian
Jopson at Aisgill, February 1983

But that is not necessarily BR's problem -- most steam-hauled excursions are run by SLOA and they contribute about £400,000-a-year towards InterCity receipts of £500m. But on the Settle-Carlisle -- the chosen route for nearly half of all steam excursions -- the run-down of services in the early 80s put steam trains in the position where they were generating enough revenue to significantly offset losses on the scheduled passenger services. Notwithstanding the caution of Mr Ward, the transport consultants PEIDA found that the market for steam excursions on the Settle-Carlisle was a remarkably buoyant one. A postal survey of those travelling on such trains revealed not only that 61 per cent would travel on the line more frequently if there were more (a third of them said they would make between two and four extra trips a year) but that 90 per cent of them would be prepared to pay an extra £2 for the privilege.

This would appear to begin to answer two of the problems at one stroke: more demand would mean higher use of trains and higher fares would mean steam engines going closer to meeting their overheads. But of course, BR was to some extent dragged kicking and screaming back into the steam age -- it is only 13 years since it succumbed to pressure and allowed SLOA limited running over more lightly used lines. The return of steam to the Settle-Carlisle was only permitted much later, in 1980, and was an immediate success. Almost 90 per cent of respondents to the PEIDA survey rated the line as the best for steam excursions and both SLOA and BR told the consultants there was scope for a substantial increase in the number of trips. PEIDA went so far as to suggest the demand was to some extent unique to the Settle-Carlisle and if the line closed, a nett reduction in the number of steam excursions on the BR network would result. PEIDA put demand at 45 excursions a year, each yielding £1,000 revenue.

But this figure looks distinctly conservative alongside the usage of privately run steam railways. Lines in the North of England include the North Yorkshire Moors and the Ravenglass and Eskdale, both of which carry about 250,000 passengers annually, and the Keighley and Worth Valley which carries about half that number. It would be hard to imagine 250,000 people cramming just 45 trains and, while the above-mentioned lines are all much shorter, there seems no good reason to doubt that the Settle-Carlisle could support a regular steam-hauled service such as that run so successfully on the heavy loss-making Fort William to Mallaig line. While, unlike most of the private railways, BR could not rely on volunteer labour for the service, neither would the steam services have to bear all the infrastructure costs.

But steam excursions are in many ways no more than aside to the debate about the future of the Settle-Carlisle. So assuming the line were to stay with us, what other services might it provide? It may seem perverse to pose the question in this way....surely rational transport planning requires that facilities be provided to meet perceived demands, rather than a demand created for a facility which just happens to be there. But that nonetheless is the reality which has resulted from BR's assessment that the Settle-Carlisle is surplus to its trunk route requirements. The other side of the coin is that there is good reason to believe that the features of the line are such that there exists a largely untapped demand which could enable the line to fulfil a far broader range of functions than that of the residual local service.

The following appraisal is constructed from research data where possible, but it should be remembered that in such complex fields as the promotion of leisure services, market research has been known to be very unreliable. On the other hand, there is a proven relationship between marketing and demand. British Rail's own experience on the Settle-Carlisle has shown that the combination of a good marketing man in Ron Cotton and wide media exposure can make even the badly timed and generally inconvenient trains still running on the line generate a healthy operating surplus. In 1985, passenger use was up 20 per cent on 1984 which in turn was 50 per cent up on 1983. Revenue was up to £1m. -- about 70 per cent higher than PEIDA thought could be achieved with the current level of service. The Yorkshire Post's Alan Whitehouse quoted a "highly-placed" BR source in London as saying: "It means that the Settle-Carlisle is one of our best performing provincial railways. It also effectively kills the suggestion that the only people using the line are railway enthusiasts taking a last trip. This is the second year of major traffic growth and all the indications are that the bulk of the passengers are families. Train buffs account for 20 per cent at most."

The embarrassingly good figures added fuel to the debate which had been simmering within BR. As Mr Cotton himself put it: "There are two schools of thought, and who is to know which is right? One says that if we change our minds and decide not to close the line, all these new passengers will just go away. The other says that people aren't just going for a last trip and if you really push the line you can increase usage." Mr Cotton is not prepared to say which school of thought he subscribes to, but the reader is invited to make an educated guess in the light of his reputation for innovation.

Of course the use of the Settle-Carlisle can not be considered in a political vacuum. As will be seen from the debate developed in the final chapter, any enhanced role for the railways in Britain must be considered very unlikely indeed in the foreseeable future -- certainly under a Tory government committed to monetarist policies. In this climate, BR has determined that the two profitable Anglo-Scottish routes (East and West Coast) are sufficient to meet the demands of InterCity and freight traffic. Both these sectors have stringent Government targets to meet. The Freight Sector comes bottom of the overheads "pecking order" and hence trunk services could be transferred to Settle-Carlisle and local freight traffic increased without the sector incurring additional costs. But the InterCity Sector is top of this pecking order and the reintroduction of such services to the line would serve, in accounting terms, only to dissipate revenue while increasing costs. Indeed, probably the whole of the infrastructure costs of the Settle-Carlisle would fall on InterCity. This means that any plan to reintroduce, for example, Nottingham to Glasgow trains over the line would have to meet a stringent test as to the revenue likely to be generated. Only a relaxation of Government targets would make this a realistic option in the short term. That does not, of course, preclude the possibility of what would effectively be an inter-city service being run by the provincial sector.

Nonetheless, nothing can alter the fact that the Settle-Carlisle offers the most direct link between two of the most highly populated conurbations in Britain -- West Yorkshire (1.8m.) and Clydeside (2m.). The timings achievable between Leeds and Carlisle via Carnforth -- as already stated -- compare very poorly even with the residual local service on the Settle-Carlisle. It is also a route over which competition from roads is at a significant time disadvantage because the A65 trunk road from Leeds to the M6 near Kendal is slow and often congested with holiday traffic.

So if the line is retained, the restoration of InterCity services would appear to be an obvious priority objective. A report commissioned by the Settle-Carlisle Joint Action Committee from Transport and Environment Studies (TEST) looks at the possibility of upgrading the line to take InterCity 125 services, with speeds of up to 100mph in line with its designed capability rather than the current 60mph limit. The trackwork costs of such a scheme are not available as this book is being written, but TEST envisages making use of existing stretches of continuous welded rail where possible, in line with PEIDA singling scheme. It seems reasonable to presume that InterCity or any similar services over the line should provide the principal service to and from the major stations currently served by the Leeds-Carlisle locals, namely Shipley (for Bradford), Keighley, Skipton, Settle and Appleby.

Other types of potential service can be broadly categorised as fulfilling either a local or a leisure need. Given the problems already described relating to the reintroduction of InterCity services, it is probably in the leisure field that the Settle-Carlisle offers the best immediate marketing possibilities. The success of the monthly DalesRail services was well documented in Chapter Two and it is to be hoped that, if it is decided the line should stay open, BR might swallow its pride and consider the possibility of reopening stations for regular use, the obvious initial choices being Kirkby Stephen and Garsdale.

One of the beauties of the Settle-Carlisle stems from its conception as a trunk rather than a local route, which means that, by and large, it does not duplicate access to the more developed parts of the Yorkshire Dales National Park. Rather, it provides speedy north-south access to the western part of the park where the number of visitors has not begun to cause problems. It has the potential significantly to increase the number of visitors to the part of the park most able to accommodate them without increasing the number of cars on the narrow Dales roads. The Countryside Commission's DalesRail studies have shown how the service can be used to introduce a degree of control to the destination of day-trippers. Clearly the line could form part of a more fundamental access scheme which aimed to discourage or actually restrict access by car to the national park's most heavily visited centres (such policies are already successfully operated in the Peak District National Park). The problems of Horton-in-Ribblesdale, where a long and bitter row split the village over national park plans to build a car park in a traditional hay meadow, springs immediately to mind. It could also help encourage ramblers away from areas where erosion is becoming a problem (the Three Peaks) to less frequented but arguably even more attractive areas like the Howgill Fells.

There have been various initiatives to establish rail/bus access to the national park which has no "full-time" stations within its boundaries. In 1979 and 80, the park committee backed an experimental Three Peaks bus service from Giggleswick station to Hawes and a Sunday service from Giggleswick to Ribblehead. The response to the latter was disappointing and it was quickly abandoned. A Tuesday and Saturday summer service from Settle to Hawes lasted until 1982. The park committee also assisted BR to the tune of £2,200 between 1978 and 1981 in promoting the Parklink integrated rail/bus service from West Yorkshire. This too was subsequently abandoned. The advent of the Dales Wayfarer -- offering through ticketing on services by BR, West Yorkshire PTE and the West Yorkshire Road Car Company -- typifies the new approach to public transport within the park. The Countryside Commission-sponsored Wayfarer Project (see Chapter Two) concentrated on the off-peak use of existing services to promote access to the park (and also to the Peak park). At the time of writing it has successfully provided an integrated service to the southern part of the park. It is possible to envisage how this policy of dovetailing existing public transport services might be developed by extending existing bus routes to Hawes from Leyburn in the east and Kendal in the west to connect with trains at Garsdale to serve a "Sedbergh-Hawes corridor".

The demise of some previous integrated transport systems in the Dales could well be related to the fact that the leg of the journey which actually takes the visitor into the park has been by bus rather than train. Using the attractions of the Settle-Carlisle as a marketing device, the line could become the spine of a Dales transport system, with short connecting bus or minibus spurs modelled on the successful DalesRail services. Links from Ribblehead (subject to arrangements to permit northbound as well as southbound trains to stop) to Ingleton and from Dent station to Dent town might be worth developing, as might a new station at Mallerstang to open up access to the upper Eden valley. This was the longest stretch without a station when the line was built, because the local people could not raise the £2,000 required by the Midland for building an access road. A halt for ramblers could be built with or without vehicle access for a relatively small sum (certainly when compared with the cost of making good the maintenance backlog). For example, British Rail has built a number of new stations to the specification of West Yorkshire PTE, to full Railway Inspectorate standards for as little as £100,000.

The likely demand for the sort of expanded DalesRail detailed above is, of course, difficult to determine and is a question which PEIDA to some extent shied away from by not giving serious consideration to the reopening of stations such as Garsdale, Kirkby Stephen and Horton-in-Ribblesdale (as advocated in the Settle-Carlisle Joint Action Committee's 1986 campaign). Nonetheless, PEIDA found "clear evidence" of "user demand for expansion" of the DalesRail service as well as a "dynamic, growing market" in which 30 per cent of 1983 users were actually making their first trip. PEIDA concluded that even an enhanced DalesRail service would generate only £10,000 a year surplus to BR. But it must be pointed out that this assumes only the continuation of the existing weekend format using trains chartered from BR by other bodies. Again other possibilities, such as greatly increased frequencies to enable longer than merely overnight stays by visitors, were not considered. Nor was the possibility of attracting more people in cars by setting up a park-and-ride service from, say, Hellifield. It is worth remembering too, that PEIDA's estimates of likely traffic on the Leeds-Carlisle service have already proved very conservative. The map gives an indication of the facilities and places of interest on or near the line.

There has also been some thought devoted to the idea of generating extra traffic on the line by means of extra development along it. One such scheme got off to a bad start when journalists latched on to its proposal for a "theme corridor" and dubbed it a "70-mile Disneyland in the Dales". In fact the idea of Sian Johnson and Associates, a London-based marketing consultancy, was to develop "major high intensity tourist magnets" at about four lineside sites with the aim of ultimately attracting a million passengers a year on ten or 12 trains a day.

With such traffic levels, the company saw the line as being self-financing and offering a major "leisure investment opportunity". Ms Johnson mentioned ideas such as a "navvy museum" to the work of the great railway builders as typifying the sort of development felt to be in keeping with the line. She drew comparison with major comparable attractions, such as the Beamish open-air industrial museum in County Durham, with 200,000 visitors a year, and the Blaenau Ffestiniog slate mines. These major magnets would be complemented by "lineside development and tourist services such as shops, pubs, amusements, indoor and evening entertainments, sporting activities, holiday accommodation (e.g. time-share cottages)", and accommodation and catering developments "off-line" in nearby towns and villages. Among companies showing interest in the scheme was hotels and restaurants giant, Imperial Leisure, and clearly a major concern of the national park, as planning authority, was -- and would remain -- the likely environmental impact of intrusive schemes on this largely unspoilt area. To put the idea into perspective, the number of annual visitors to the Upper Dales Folk Museum in Hawes is just 20,000.

Ms Johnson said in December 1985 that the scheme had not been dropped but was merely "on ice" pending the outcome of the closure hearings. Meanwhile her consultancy has formed the Settle-Carlisle Railway Company Ltd. and an associated marketing company ready to spring into action once the line's fate is known. "We can go with either BR or a private line," she said. It is understood that a decision to close the line would rekindle ideas for a privately run railway first mooted by the Carnforth-based Steamtown museum which is also one of the major operators of steam locomotives on BR tracks. Ms Johnson said there had been "cordial" talks with the national park committee on possible development. Her company has also set up a "data base" comprising the country's top 600 tourist attractions and is working on the market research of leisure attractions to help the industry understand why some ventures succeed while others, such as the Britannia British Genius theme park in Derbyshire, are dramatic failures.

A very much less controversial scheme to increase the use of the Settle-Carlisle through tourist development was prepared for the Countryside Commission by the Centre for Environmental Interpretation at Manchester Polytechnic. This envisaged a gradual build-up of use of the line through an extended DalesRail-type service, towards 400,000 passengers a year. The research team's suggestions were contained in a report entitled Interpreting the Heritage of the Settle-Carlisle Railway Line, "interpreting" being a word chosen to describe the more participative type of educational day out which is seen as one of the ways leisure time use should be going in the 80s. The team saw this interpretation as the last piece in the jig-saw which could bring the Settle-Carlisle alive for visitors.

"The conservation and appreciation of our natural and man-made heritage has rightly become big business in Britain, with many millions of people taking leisure trips each year. In

1983 the value and volume of tourism to England increased substantially with 121 million trips and £7,600m.-worth of expenditure. There has been a substantial increase in visiting places of interest, particularly where these offer an opportunity to glimpse into the past. The present rate of change in British society is remarkable and as manufacturing employment is replaced by a leisure and service economy this is giving more people the time and the inclination to discover their natural and man-made heritage on leisure trips and visits."

The report identified a number of themes which could be developed for the interest of rail users and others through booklets, self-guided trails and displays. Themes for self-guided trails, combined with displays at the appropriate stations included limestone scenery and quarrying at Horton; the navvy towns at Ribblehead; upland landscape and land-use at Dent; town trails and the development of settlements at Appleby, Kirkby Stephen and Settle; agriculture and land-use in the Eden Valley at Langwathby. The report suggested a more ambitious plan for Garsdale station, where there would be a visitor centre, possibly housed in converted railway carriages which could be used for a travelling exhibition in winter. Like Settle and Appleby, the station should be restored to its original Midland Victorian splendour to "create a feeling of a working museum". The polytechnic group envisaged that such a centre would attract about 30,000 visitors a year. Also suggested in the report were observation cars on trains, with "on-board interpretation", and an annual railway festival.

Although the Manchester scheme, unlike the Sian Johnson one, would clearly be unlikely to raise significant environmental objections, both ideas are variations on the same theme. This theme is the recognition that the Settle-Carlisle line is an important part of Britain's national heritage which should remain, in use, for the enjoyment and education of ourselves and our children. But creating some kind of working museum should not be seen as an end in itself. Increased tourist usage could also bring benefits to communities which might not otherwise be able to support their own rail service.

The problems of stimulating economic activity in remote upland areas and stemming the outward flow of young people are complex ones which have yet to be addressed successfully (see A Better Future for the Uplands, published by the Countryside Commission, 1984). The "easy answer" of promoting tourism undoubtedly brings considerable sums of money into areas like the Dales, but the benefits tend to flow most freely to those with capital to exploit them, namely people from more affluent parts of the country who can afford to buy up and renovate hotels and restaurants. The disbenefits of tourism include the inflation of the property market by owners of second homes and holiday lets so that young local people are priced out, traffic congestion, depressed wage levels and seasonal fluctuation in the jobs market.

Attempts to stimulate light manufacturing industries by building small industrial units have been conspicuously unsuccessful -- a £250,000 seven-unit development at Hawes has still provided no jobs at the time of writing, almost three years after its completion. The answer would appear to lie in the fact the upper dales are remote from potential markets and they do not have a large and ready pool of job-hungry unemployed people. It is not unemployment so much as lack of varied and challenging employment which lies behind the perceived exodus of young people. But a rejuvenated railway could bring very real social benefits to the upland areas through which it passes. The Settle-Carlisle -- connecting the heads of so many of the remoter dales -- could become an alternative economic magnet to counter the traditional pull of the larger centres down the the dales... a pull which exerts itself on the Dales population in all fields from education, to business, to recreation.

Stimulating economic activity beside the line could actually create a reason for travelling up rather than down dale, while at the same time opening up a new, all-weather north-south travel axis to help alleviate the economic problems associated with isolation. The railway could become a vital part of a plan to stimulate the sort of "brain" rather than "brawn"-based economic activity which is beginning to be found in other rural areas, such as mid-Wales. The upper dales are geographically central to about 15 million people in the north of England and the suggestion has been made that some regionally-based operations such as architects' practices, computer programmers or small laboratories might find not inconsiderable improvements in their working environment and productivity by relocating to the Dales. One has in mind industries in which the cost of transporting a finished product is not an important consideration but to which existing road communications difficulties are nonetheless a deterrent.

It will be appreciated that plans for the future of the Settle-Carlisle are necessarily hedged with many ifs and buts which would not be removed simply by a decision not to close the line -- that would hopefully be only the beginning of concerted action by BR, local authorities, the Yorkshire Dales National Park and other statutory bodies to exploit the line to its obvious potential for the benefit of both visitors and local people. The following, therefore, is intended only to present ideas for discussion as to the range of services the line might carry.

☐ Long distance expresses, e.g. Nottingham to Glasgow -- subject to the constraints already mentioned -- stopping at Settle and Appleby.

☐ Semi-fast services connecting destinations such as Hull, York, Bradford and East Lancashire with Carlisle and South-West Scotland and stopping additionally at Kirkby Stephen and Garsdale, from where there would be connecting minibus services to Hawes and Sedbergh.

☐ Journey-to-work services -- possibly as part of the above -- to fulfil a need identified by surveys for the Settle-Carlisle Joint Action Committee, at Horton-in-Ribblesdale and to connect the expanding "dormitory" Eden valley villages with Carlisle.

☐ Summer ramblers' DalesRail type services calling at all existing halts.

☐ Park-and-ride services -- probably linked with the above -- to and from Hellifield and, possibly at a later date, from a station at the northern end of the line.

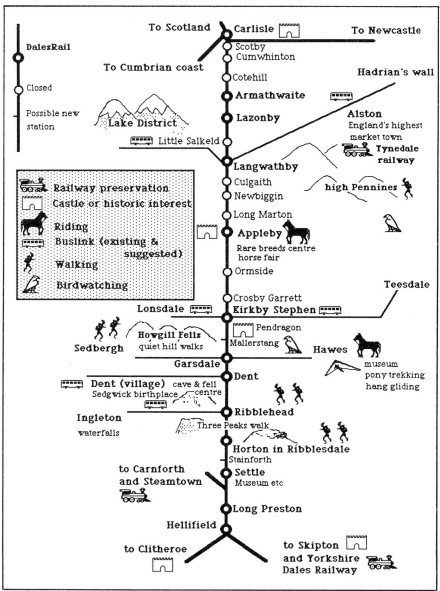

Map of the Settle-Carlisle line showing nearby attractions and
possible developments.

145

☐ Steam-hauled specials and "heritage" trains with observation coaches, on-board commentary and catering which would travel at no more than 30mph, so as to permit appreciation of the panoramas. It is possible to envisage Orient Express-style rail tours taking in the Settle-Carlisle along with, say, the West Highland route. Sadly, the obvious scenic route north from Carlisle, via the the Waverley line, is now lost. Obviously such tourist orientated services would need to be carefully balanced so the one did not simply steal trade from the other. The idea of a one-way steam-hauled trip and a "heritage" return, or vice versa, would seem a marketable package.

Various people have mooted restoring services on other railways in the area of the Settle-Carlisle. Clearly the viability of such costly exercises would depend on the success or otherwise of the sort of Settle-Carlisle rejuvenation ideas described. In many ways, however, the branch lines lack some of the obvious attractions of the main line, both from a scenic point of view and because they tend to serve places already nearing their tourist capacity. The restoration of rail links in Wensleydale or, perhaps more realistically, from Appleby to Penrith and Keswick, should probably only be promoted as a means of controlling access by road.

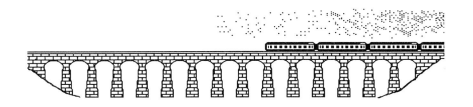

10. The loaded dice

"GOOD evening. Here is the news. The Gravelly Hill interchange on the M6 at Birmingham is to close. The Minister of Transport today announced his decision which follows the lengthy public inquiry into the future of the so-called Spaghetti Junction on the motorway which links the M1 with the north-west of England. The closure plan, which has been bitterly contested by the AA, the RAC and the Road Haulage Association, is aimed at saving an annual repair bill running into hundreds of millions of pounds on the interchange and the associated section of elevated motorway.

"The Minister said the spending of Department of Transport funds on a defective structure whose design standards were inadequate for its actual loads could no longer be justified. Traffic will be diverted to the south of Birmingham via the M42, a detour of 15 miles. Today's controversial announcement brings the row about Britain's roads into the urban areas for the first time -- it follows the publication last week of the Rural Roads White Paper which proposes the closure of 20,000 miles of unclassified road to avoid duplication, and the withdrawal of winter snow clearance and gritting operations on roads serving communities of fewer than 500 people."

The above broadcast is, of course, fictitious and clearly absurd. Whatever the mistakes of civil engineering in the 60s and 70s in pushing materials beyond their limits and of the 80s in sending ever heavier lorries over the structures that resulted, there can be little logic in dismembering the national motorway and trunk road network. And yet by the same token it ought to be considered just as illogical to carve chunks -- like the Settle-Carlisle -- out of the trunk rail network, even if most of the rural branches have already gone the way of the country roads in our make-believe news bulletin. Chapter Three told how the Ministry of Transport became, effectively, the Ministry of Roads. But what is the economic and political machinery which assures the continued pre-eminence of road transport to the obvious detriment of rail?

It is surprisingly difficult to produce a wholly accurate picture of Government and local authority spending on the 200,000-odd miles of public roads in Britain. This is not because of any cover-up or massaging of figures by the DTp -- it is simply not easy to determine precisely what proportion of, for example, civil service and local authority staff costs should be attributed to spending on roads. Working from DTp figures, spending on road building and maintenance in 1984-5 can be put at £2,899m, according to Kerry Hamilton, co-author of Losing Track. The trunk road and motorway network accounts for rather less than ten per cent of the total mileage, but -- carrying a substantial proportion of the traffic -- it swallows £1,020m, or 35 per cent of the spending. An increasing proportion of that sum is attributable to maintenance, as many motorways now need rebuilding -- a piece in The Observer of August 8, 1985, quoted the Auditor General, Sir Gordon Downey, as saying £175m was necessary for "urgent and vital motorway repairs". The newspaper suggested the alarming decline of bridges and structures ("concrete cancer" being the latest cause) would make this sum look like "small change".

Against this, vehicle excise duty raised £2,219m in 1984-5 and VAT on petrol etcetera £2,850m, according to a Parliamentary answer to a question from an Edinburgh MP, Ron Brown. The DTp estimates that all forms of taxation on road users yielded £11,619m in 1984, of which £9,412m was attributed to private motorists (who would be unable to reclaim VAT or offset duty against tax).

This quite enormous revenue figure would seem on the face of it to cover road costs threefold. But there are a number of other costs attributable to the roads. For example, there is the "subsidy" to company cars (half the new car market) represented by tax concessions to both the driver and the company. Hamilton and Potter put this at £1,500m a year. Then there is the cost of accidents. The DTp currently puts the cost of a fatal accident to the emergency and hospital services and to society at large at around £170,000. If we allow for the fact that each fatal accident probably represents more than one fatality, then the cost of the 7,000 annual road deaths will be about £1,000m (a figure which probably does not adequately reflect the true "cost" to society of the loss of individuals in which it has "invested" by means of education and training). Add in the cost of other accidents and the equation does at least begin to look a little more balanced.

But in many ways even trying to balance the equation is to be drawn up a blind alley. After all, the Exchequer collects a lot of revenue from VAT on the sale of refrigerators and record players -- it does not feel obliged to plough these monies back into the electrical industry. By the same token it would appear specious to argue that revenue from, for example, VAT on the sale of cars and motor accessories -- which is really incidental to the roads programme -- should be counted in the equation alongside vehicle excise duty. A more illuminating approach is to compare the way in which investment decisions on rail or road schemes are made within the Department of Transport.

Ostensibly, investment in roads is designed to meet the demand created by the increasing number of vehicles on them and investment calculations are necessarily based on estimates of vehicle ownership growth. These estimates have tended, over the years, to be somewhat inflated, often grossly so, being based on assumptions of sustained economic growth. For example, the Transport and Road Research Laboratory in 1967 forecast 0.6 cars per person by 2010. Ten years later it was accepted that 0.45 cars per person would represent "saturation level". Today there are about 20 million vehicles on our roads, or about a third of a car each. Put another way, 60 per cent of households own or have the use of a car, a figure which disguises the fact that outside the prosperous South-East the figure is frequently, if not generally, below 50 per cent (as in West Yorkshire for example).

But car ownership by no means guarantees mobility for all members of a household. Personal Mobility and Transport Policy by Mayer Hillman, Irwin Henderson and Anne Whalley (1973) is particularly revealing as to the level of access to a car enjoyed by various groups of people and is summarised by Hamilton and Potter thus: "....the use of a car, even in a car-owning household, tends to be very selective. Cars are predominatly used by adult men and the travel needs of other household members fitted around their wishes."

Research findings by Hillman and Whalley quoted earlier in this book showed that even car owners frequently preferred the train for certain journeys. An effect of road investment is to improve the quality of journeys by car, thereby shifting the threshold at which rail travel is likely to be the preferred option. Thus road investment will tend to generate increased traffic, leading in turn to demand for further investment. A classic case is the opening by 1985 of most sections of the M25 London orbital motorway on which traffic is reportedly way above forecast levels. For some years British Rail had been seeking sanction for its scheme to build or reopen cross-London InterCity links which might arguably have met some of the traffic demands now being fulfilled by the motorway.

Of course the more road investment encourages a switch to the private car, the less demand there is for public transport which consequently enters the all too familiar spiral of decline of increased fares, reduced frequencies and facilities and rising demand for subsidy.

Road investment in Britain, in the continued absence of any discernible national transport policy, seems to be fuelled as much by its own momentum as any serious economic consideration -- in a Department of Transport dominated by highway engineers there is a very clear vested professional interest in sustaining current levels of road investment. Trunk roads cost upwards of £2m-a-mile to build depending on the width of the road, its location and the nature of the terrain to be crossed (the issue which prompted Ron Brown's question was the proposal to spend up to £100m on a mile or so of Western Relief Road in the Scottish capital). The method used for assessing the value of a particular investment is dictated by the fact that the revenue received from users of the new facility can not be directly attributed to it. So the DTp in most cases uses a computer programme called COBA to run a cost/benefit appraisal of road schemes which takes into account factors such as reduced accident levels and time saved compared with a "do nothing" approach. Schemes are expected to show a 15 per cent return on investment in the first year's operation.

British Rail investment plans, on the other hand, can be subjected to a very much simpler test as services on given stretches of railway are funded directly by ticket sales. BR plans are nearly always assessed according to the simple method of financial appraisal -- in broad terms this means that any investment must pay for itself in cash-flow terms. Thus the major £306m scheme to electrify the East Coast main line finally won DTp approval because BR presented a case which showed that consequent savings in loco maintenance and operating costs outweighed the increased infrastructure maintenance and the investment cost. This might a first glance seem fair enough -- after all it is only the type of test which private enterprises apply all the time to investment proposals. But, rightly or wrongly, private companies need not generally concern themselves with the effect their own investments have on other companies or society at large.

British Rail, on the other hand, is part of the Government-run infrastructure of Britain and the external costs and benefits of schemes are of direct interest to us all. Yet in practice, the cost/benefit technique is generally only used in connection with rail **closure** proposals and not with investment plans. Even then it is only ancilliary to financial appraisal. Studies have shown (British Rail Board/ P. Mackie, 1973) that the financial return of a scheme will rarely exceed the return expressed in cost/benefit terms. Indeed the only occasion when such an outcome is really possible is when there are two directly competing modes of transport over a particular route and investment in one may attract customers for the other without any broader benefits.

It should come as no surprise, then, that there are many ostensibly worthwhile rail schemes which are never enacted because they fail to meet to narrow financial criteria laid down. In other countries cost/benefit analysis is widely used to assess investment proposals. In France, for example, plans to improve the line from Paris to Clermont Ferrand would have yielded a financial return of just 1.5 per cent. The cost/ benefit return, by contrast, was some 28 per cent. Even in that bastion of free enterprise and road transport, the United States, a cost/benefit study on the Boston-Washington corridor led to the decision to invest $2,000m in the railroads. In West Germany all rail, road and water proposals are evaluated by means of a cost/effectiveness appraisal which "scores" benefits in points and puts schemes in a priority order to avoid competition and to ensure the three modes complement each other where possible. Thus if there is a high speed railway alongside the route of a proposed motorway this duplication will reduce the "points value" of the road scheme and make it less likely to show a positive return.

In Britain, by contrast, road and rail schemes are processed through different hierarchies at the DTp and comparable schemes are never looked at side by side. There have been a few cases of cost/benefit analysis on rail investment schemes in Britain, such as those that led to the retention of the Manchester to Hadfield and Glossop lines in 1974. More recently, a study was carried out by the Transport and Road Research Laboratory, Newcastle University, Tyne and Wear County Council and Tyne and Wear PTE into the effect of the opening of the Metro integrated rapid transit system. The light electric railway was built on Tyneside partly as an alternative to major investment in urban motorways. The Metro Report showed the system had yielded an estimated return of eight per cent on nett capital cost in its first year. Even given low economic growth the system would give a social return of 73 per cent over 30 years -- more or less equivalent to the financial return which would have been obtained by the average private sector investor. Significantly it led to a major rise in public transport usage among both car and non-car owners and consequently also yielded benefits to motorists through reduced congestion leading to shorter journey times.

Such analyses, sadly, remain the exception and the DTp juggernaut rolls relentlessly on. It is aided in its progress by political ignorance and dogma. The juggernaut is fuelled not only by overt lobbyists like the British Road Federation, but almost inadvertently by countless other interest groups. This is because of the commonly held belief that building roads creates employment for the area in question. There is mounting economic evidence that this is far from being the case and a growing body of academic opinion holds that the very opposite could be true. The case is that building roads to serve depressed areas merely makes it easier to transport goods to those areas from areas which are already advantaged. Far from creating new jobs in depressed areas, road-building could well cost jobs as local warehousing facilities are rendered redundant by fewer, centralised units. Juggernauts effectively act as warehouses on wheels as large companies find they can serve the whole country from a couple of strategically located "giant" facilities, one, say, near the M25 and the other near the M62.

Yet MPs of all persuasions continue to join in the lobbying and bartering process which helps decide which areas get the new roads. And countless local pressure groups add their weight by campaigning for bypasses which, while probably bringing local environmental improvement, have the nett effect of exacerbating problems at the next bottleneck. The Press, by indulging the pronouncements of politicians and industrialists, helps foster the consensus view. Even a quality newspaper like The Guardian felt moved to publish recently 58 column centimetres of unrestrained road lobby bigotry by one George Bishop, who argued among other things for a "road supremo" with power to override all objectors to road schemes to enable a road-building programme as "a classic solution for unemployment".

Given this general acceptance by an inadequately-informed populace of the case for roads (provided, that is, that they are not built through our own back garden or our local pub) it is hardly surprising that gestures towards putting road and rail investment appraisal on an equal footing have come to nothing. For example, the Advisory Committee on Trunk Road Assessment under its chairman Sir George Leitch produced a report in 1977 aimed at standardising assessment of road and rail schemes. While the Leitch Report implicitly rejected the DTp view that there was "no obvious bias" in favour of roads because of the different assessment methods, it accepted that financial appraisal was probably not appropriate for assessing road schemes. But it saw no good reason why the cost/benefit analysis applied to trunk road appraisal should not be adapted for rail once the terms had been standardised between the two (for example, "investment" in roads means, effectively, building new roads whereas in railways it encompasses what might more properly be termed maintenance or renewal). Further, the Leitch Report felt the cost/benefit appraisal system applied to roads was unnecessarily dominated by factors which could be expressed in money terms and it strongly implied that not enough consideration was given to such as environmental factors.

This theme was developed further for the DTp in a study by Colin Buchanan and Partners who applied cost/benefit techniques to a notional investment in electrifying the Coventry-Oxford-Reading routes to the South Coast and Paddington. Critics argue the study was so constrained by having to use the COBA model that its results were of questionable value. So there seems no good reason to believe there is any immediate likelihood of the financial appraisal method of assessing rail investment being abandoned in favour of a fairer system. Indeed a recent Appeal Court judgement would seem to reinforce the notion that the DTp is under no obligation whatsoever to consider alternatives to its road proposals. The Department won its case, with costs, against the veteran anti-motorway campaigner Helen Anscomb who claimed it had not given adequate reason for approving a route for the M40 Oxford-Birmingham motorway between Banbury and Gaydon. "We were asked by counsel for ministers to put alternative strategies," Miss Anscomb told The Guardian, referring to the public inquiry procedure. "We should have been told at the beginning that they were not prepared to put money into rail."

But Lord Justice Purchas said ministers had given ample reasons for their decision to approve the scheme. In a remarkably revealing statement he said the duty of the inquiry was not to establish the best of a number of alternatives, but merely to inform ministers about objections and obtain the inspector's view.

Within the general framework which mitigates against rail investment, BR is subject to fluctuating political whims according to which party is in power and, indeed, to which wing of the party in power holds the greatest sway. BR's blackest period in recent years followed the election of the Conservatives under Mrs Thatcher -- an assessment readily confirmed for me by the former BR chairman, Sir Peter Parker, when he said bluntly: "The first Thatcher Government didn't like the railways." For him, the turning came with the Serpell Report which was "an aberration" marking the "last effort" to thwart the railways. "David Serpell was a good and loyal member of the Railways Board but his committee was appointed for him without any consultation with us and he got lumbered with a committee which broke up under him. I wanted a neutral report which could help David Howell see the railway case, but Goldstein spoiled the Serpell Report."

With BR's defeat of ASLEF in the flexible rostering dispute, the departure of some of the Prime Minister's closest and most extreme advisers, and her election for a second term, the outlook improved, said Sir Peter. And the investment seeds sown under his chairmanship (which began under the Labour Government) finally began to bear fruit under Sir Bob Reid, with the go-ahead for East Coast electrification, the cross-London links and the Channel Tunnel.

But approval for a few schemes does not in itself provide stable conditions for planning: "Railways are a long term industry with a great future," said Sir Peter. "For us five years is short-term planning but it's an eternity for a politician. Generally speaking, the country has not got a knack of taking long-term decisions and railways have suffered terribly from that. Because railways go on and don't suddenly hit the buffers they suffer from what I call the crumbling edge of quality." This is the problem epitomised by the Government's determination continually to cut back on the PSO grant -- the subsidy to the Provincial Sector which includes the Settle-Carlisle line. "You can't have it both ways," said Sir Peter. "You can't sustain the system at the same size immutably and go on cutting back on the Government contract -- the difficulties pile up and one was eventually able to see the enormous backlog building up on track maintenance and in the age of the trains."

On the general question of the assessment of rail versus road investment, Sir Peter said it was "ridiculous" and "absurd" that social costs were not considered in rail plans. But he rejected notions of an outright conspiracy against rail. "Of course there are lobbies, but if you start playing cops and robbers you have to begin with the assumption that you have a transport policy which someone knows something about. We don't have that in Britain, so the fight is continually against vested interests." And among those interests was the DTp itself, he said. "Part of the problem is that when an economy is not planned, you end up with huge bureaucracies -- and bureaucracies consist of unenterprising people."

Not even the National Economic Development Council looked at overall transport policy, said Sir Peter. "There is no watching brief for transport policy in this country and and it's for that reason you get into these stale wars between the rubber wheel and the steel wheel when really there is a commonwealth of transport." He concluded: "I don't think it's a conspiracy -- it's just a cock-up."

Conclusion

SO -- where does all this leave the Settle-Carlisle line? Hopefully this book will have demonstrated that the future of these 72 miles of trunk route can not be seen in isolation from the position of the railway network generally. Perhaps the reader will also have concluded that decisions on transport in Britain are still taken today in much the same way as they were a hundred years ago -- in the absence of any clear national policy. In these circumstances, the theoretical basis for the ministerial decision on the line's future lies in the likely harship closure would cause. The first of the TUCC hearings to assess that hardship is just ten weeks away at the time of writing. But it will take some months for the TUCCs to report to the Minister and several more for the Minister to reach his decision.

There is no real evidence to suggest, however, that the decision on the Settle-Carlisle will be based any more on the question of hardship than other such decisions have been in the past. The real criteria on which the outcome of closure proceedings depend are political ones or, occasionally, over-riding questions of national interest, such as defence. (It is not too surprising that many remote lines which have escaped closure serve important defence installations -- the Kyle and Cumbrian coast lines spring immediately to mind -- and it is at the behest of the Ministry of Defence that there are no plans to close the Settle-Carlisle north of Appleby from where a branch serves the Warcop firing ranges and munitions stores.)

The Settle-Carlisle has become a live and significant political question and a decision either way could have important repercussions for the Government. It is not simply a Left-Right issue: the problem for Tory MPs in rural constituencies throughout Britain is epitomised by John Watson (Skipton and Ripon) who lodged the very first objection to the proposed closure. The problem for the Government is to reconcile the closure of the Settle-Carlisle with the oft repeated assurance that there is no general threat to rural railways in all the other Tory shire seats with even more highly subsidised lines. And on the line itself there is not one Tory-held seat which could not be termed marginal in the current climate of three-party politics.

In short, then, a decision to close the line this side of the next General Election could well be Government suicide. Of course a decision could be made to retain the line. But by implication that would leave the Government to address the thorny problem of the PSO grant in more generous and constructive manner should it be re-elected. Far more likely is a delaying strategy to ensure the Settle-Carlisle question is the first to address the mind of the incoming Secretary of State, whatever his or her political colour, after the General Election in 1987 or 1988.

So supposing it is decided to retain the line? How can it be ensured that the whole grisly run-down and closure process does not begin anew? This book has hopefully demonstrated that there is indeed a future for the line once the necessary investment in its structures is made. But again this can not be seen in isolation from the position of the railways as a whole. The most urgent questions to be addressed are the level of support to the various British Rail sectors. It is no good Secretary of State Nicholas Ridley (or his successor) calling for no route closures on the one hand and reliable, attractive and punctual services on the other -- all while lopping off seven per cent in Government support each year. Nor is it any good setting targets for BR sectors only to impose yet tougher targets just as the original ones were coming into sight -- like moving the goal as the team is about to score, as one writer in Modern Railways magazine put it.

At the same time, the anomalies in what is seen as the otherwise desirable sector management system need to be ironed out so they do not militate against choosing the best routes for services and offering variety of services. Increased resources on their own would go a long towards achieving this end.

What is required is an acceptance in Britain in line with that abroad that the subsidy to rail represents good value for money. The consultants, TEST (Transport and Environment Studies), calculated the cost in subsidy and social cost per passenger-kilometre for rail and road in Britain and arrived at figures of 1.9p and 2.2p respectively (BR: A European Railway, 1984). Given that in 1980 the respective gross journey figures were 36,000m and 422,000m, the absolute difference in cost between road and rail can be considerable. If those 422,000m road passenger kilometres had been provided by rail, for example, there would have been a theoretical saving of more than £1,000m. Britain's European partners recognise this value and the levels both of support to railways and of investment in them is consistently far higher than in Britain. For example, the Government in 1983 was meeting 29 per cent of BR's capital and running costs, compared with 39 per cent by the West German government, 45 per cent in France and 68 per cent in Italy. Unlike Britain, its European partners are investing significantly in railways -- in West Germany rail takes some 29.1 per cent of the transport investment budget or almost 75 per cent of the amount spent on roads. In Britain the equivalent figure is only about 7.5 per cent. Unlike Britain, its European partners generally encourage the transport of freight by rail -- in France 42 per cent of freight is carried by rail.

Unlike Britain, its European partners use more meaningful methods of appraising the value of investments as part of long-term transport objectives. Some use cost/benefit analysis, often taking into account a wide variety of social costs and benefits. Some, like Italy and the Netherlands, recognise that even the cost/benefit mathematical models can be inaccurate and rely instead on qualitative rather than quantitative assessments, within budget limits. There is much to commend such an approach.

One day, even Britain's oil will begin to run out -- standard forms of cost/benefit analysis make no allowance for the fact that rail is a far more energy-efficient than road transport. Nor do they normally take account of other resources lost through road-building (agricultural yield and many amenities which are far more difficult to quantify). Nor is there any allowance for the fact that road transport in Britain is our single greatest atmospheric pollutant, depositing 8.946m tonnes of carbon monoxide, hydrocarbons, nitrogen oxides, sulphur dioxide and smoke into the atmosphere annually. The railways' annual contribution to pollution is just 67,000 tonnes. There is currently no mechanism for attributing the cost of making good pollution damage to the activity which causes it. This is in part at least due to the fact that much of Britain's pollution problem is perceived to be "exported" to Scandinavia and Germany by the prevailing winds. There is no easy mechanism for assessing the cost of the increasing environmental and structural damage caused by ever heavier juggernauts. The DTp is currently researching urgently the mechanics of Victorian and earlier arches to assess the conditions under which they begin to fail, a question BR might have liked answering some time ago!

There are two major obstacles in the way of establishing a progressive long-term transport policy in Britain. One is the relatively short-term one represented by the present Government which, notwithstanding the shift perceived by Sir

Peter Parker, remains ideologically committed to road transport. This is reflected in many ways -- from the sanctioning of ever heavier juggernauts; to allowing lorry-based coal shipments to power stations; to bus and coach deregulation; to the abolition of the metropolitan counties with their powerful transport role. It is a philosophy which can increasingly be seen as emanating from the top, from an autocratic Premier who is quite unfamiliar with the inside of trains and who applauds the "freedom" offered by the car (never mind the lack of freedom suffered by the majority of the population without immediate access to one). In short, the road industry remains one of the few in which there is still scope to fulfil the old Tory "get-rich-quick" dream.

The other obstacle remains the Department of Transport itself, whose predisposition towards road transport has already been demonstrated. In the face of this, successive Governments of both main persuasions have appeared incapable of forging an immutable policy for the common good.

It is the belief of this author that only radical action to remove transport from the party political sphere once and for all can return us to the post-War hope of the National Transport Board, and achieve for Britain a rational transport policy to offer its citizens maximum mobility at the least possible cost. To achieve such a change would require a monumental act of political will to overcome decades of entrenchment by interest groups. It would demand the behind-the-scenes forging of political deals. It might involve the playing off of various road pressure groups against one another; holding out the prospect of new jobs in revitalised, integrated public transport systems as the sweetener for job losses in road haulage and car building. But that governments **can** achieve difficult goals, given the will, has surely been demonstrated by Mrs Thatcher's determined assault on the steel and coal unions, so carefully planned backstage in deals with such as non-union road hauliers.

The bureaucratic arm to transform the political objective into reality could be a new National Transport Executive comprising the best brains from successful municipal undertakings, academics and more progressive elements of the Civil Service. Within this body responsible for overall transport policy, a "pruned" Department of Transport could continue to exercise its existing role of processing road building schemes in line with that policy. Such a new agency -- which could be accountable to the public through some mechanism external to party government -- might usefully be located well away from the stultifying influences of Whitehall, perhaps on Tyneside where it could continually be reminded of the benefits of an efficient transport system!

This book, therefore, takes the pessimistic view insofar as it is assumed that real improvement in -- or even the sustainment of -- our rail network can only be achieved by means of major change in our institutions. The optimistic footnote to that is that if enough people can be persuaded of the merits of such change they have it within their power to help achieve it -- by campaigning through the existing pressure groups, through their trades unions, through political parties, through their councils, their MPs, the Press. The Settle-Carlisle campaign has shown the fight crosses traditional political boundaries. But whatever the outcome of the Settle-Carlisle battle, it is just that....a battle won or lost. There remains a war to be fought!

Useful contacts:

Friends of the Settle-Carlisle Line Association, c/o Peter Lawrence, Scar Garth, Church Street, Giggleswick, Settle, North Yorkshire, BD24 0BE. Tel (072 92) 2696.
Settle Carlisle Joint Action Committee, White Cross, Lancaster LA1 4XH. Tel. (0524) 388525.
Transport 2000, Walkden House, 10 Melton Street, Euston, London NW1 2EJ. Tel 01 388 8386.
Railway Development Society, BM/RDS, London WC1N 3XX. Tel. 01 405 0463.
Friends of the Earth, 377 City Road, London EC1V 1NA. Tel. 01 837 0731.
TUCC for North-East England, Record House, Bootham, York YO3 7DQ. Tel. (0904) 25615.
TUCC for the North-Western Area, Room 106, Royal Exchange, Cross Street, Manchester, M2 7BR. Tel. 061 834 5245.

Index
(principal references only)